MUSEUM of AMERICAN FINANCE

Henry J. Heinz
A Biography

Henry J. Heinz

Henry J. Heinz
A Biography

By
E. D. McCafferty
Formerly
Private Secretary to Henry J. Heinz

1st Edition, MCMXXIII
2nd Edition, MCMXXXVI
3rd Edition, MCMXXXIX
4th Edition, MCMXLII

Copyright 1923

TABLE OF CHAPTERS

		Page
	Preface	11
I.	The America of His Boyhood	17
II.	Lessons of Home	29
III.	The Dignity of Labor	37
IV.	Early Business Ventures	53
V.	The First Partnership	67
VI.	A Period of Trouble	77
VII.	Building Anew	87
VIII.	The Business Record	99
IX.	Elements of His Personality	109
X.	An Enduring Structure	127
XI.	Business Policies	137
XII.	Home and the Family Fireside	151
XIII.	Travel: A Revealer of Character	163
XIV.	Collecting Art and Antiques	177
XV.	Religion and Sunday School Work	189
XVI.	Citizen	209
XVII.	Reading the Record	225

LIST OF ILLUSTRATIONS

	Facing Page
Henry J. Heinz	5
The Mother of Henry J. Heinz	29
The Home in Sharpsburg which Henry J. Heinz Built for His Father	65
The First Desk used by Mr. Heinz in Sharpsburg, 1869	71
Mr. and Mrs. Henry J. Heinz on their Wedding Trip	81
The Board of Directors of H. J. Heinz Company, 1919	95
The Main Plant at Pittsburgh Built Up by Henry J. Heinz	99
Experience and Getting Experience—Henry J. Heinz and His Three Sons	129
Heinz Ocean Pier, Atlantic City	145
Birthplace of Henry J. Heinz	155
"Greenlawn," Residence of Henry J. Heinz, Pittsburgh	155
Mrs. Henry J. Heinz	161
The House in Sharpsburg where the Business was Started	177

LIST OF ILLUSTRATIONS
(*Continued*)

	Facing Page
The House where the Business was Started Being Moved from Sharpsburg to Pittsburgh	177
Henry J. Heinz with Cradle Roll Representatives at State Sunday School Convention, York, Penna., 1916	193
Sarah Heinz House, Built by Henry J. Heinz as a Memorial to His Wife	209
Dinner Tendered to Henry J. Heinz on His Seventieth Birthday	225
Memorial Erected by Employees of H. J. Heinz Company in Memory of the Founder	231

Preface

THIS is the biography of a man who did not seek power, or aspire to eminence above his fellow men. He took up the duties that lay next to his hand. He accepted the world as he found it; and he left it better where he touched it, not by trying to make epochal changes in it, but because, day by day, in the daily work of the common life, he thought of his neighbor. Therefore, this book is largely a record of simple deeds. He himself would have wished it to be so, for his spirit was a spirit of reverence for the simple things of daily life. It was his pride that he had tried to do a few common things a little better than they had been done before. He succeeded in doing many common things uncommonly well. He succeeded in doing many uncommon things. He built a business whose activities extend around the world. He earned wealth. He received public honors, in his own native land of America and abroad. But when he died he was the same Henry J. Heinz whom men had learned to love and respect when he was young. There was a quality in him that was no more to be disturbed by success than it had been disturbed by adversity. In the end, as in the beginning, it never occurred to him to deal with any man in terms of relative wealth, relative position. He appraised men with his heart as well as his head; and he was not afraid of the decision of his heart. He was not afraid to trust men. He believed in them. So, without striving to be a reformer of mankind, without perplexing himself with involved schemes of democracy or economic relations, he entered life anew every morning, tranquilly content each day to do what is expressed in a proverb of his mother's people: "Pick up what God has laid at the door."

He stopped to speak to children, not because he had set theories about it, but because a child was something to be loved—one of his little things of life. He stopped to speak to men laboring on the streets, not because he was trying to be democratic, but because he was Henry J. Heinz, to whom every man was worth while. He did not have to

PREFACE

cultivate democracy. It was not a condescending phrase with him. He never thought of himself except as just one of the people of the land that he loved.

And a wonderful thing came to pass. This simple man, who wrote no books about world-reform, who made no impassioned efforts to change earth's history, who with a simple spirit simply did his best in the daily personal contacts during the day's work, made an ever-widening ripple. His death came in a period when humanity had fed so heavily on tragedies and bitterness that death was a commonplace to all the world. Yet when the news of his passing went forth, men in Asia and Europe and from one end of America to the other grieved with a sense of deep loss. One of his relatives was on a ship in strange seas among men of many races. A man of the crew came to him and said: "He was a passenger on a ship where I was employed. He never passed me without saying something to me that made me feel I was somebody. There was something that did me good just in the way he would say 'Good morning.'"

PREFACE

How did Henry J. Heinz do this great thing—to make thousands of men say that they were better for his having lived? During his life, and especially during the latter part of his life, the world had seen many men do great things in many dramatic ways. He had not staged his deeds in drama. He had not sought the great deed. He accomplished what he did, because, content, he followed the promptings of an unspoiled heart. He did the little things; and lo, the days of the little things became long years, and everywhere, wherever he had trod, he had left a benediction, if it were no more than a kind word. No more than a kind word? Henry J. Heinz gave many things; but the crown of each was in the words that accompanied the gift.

These stamped his giving, not as benefactions from rich to poor, not as philanthropies dictated by the brain alone, not as mere duties that a prosperous man owes to others, not as liberalities from an employer to employees, but as the giving of a friend to friends, as the loving deed of a brother to brothers. And in this is the creed for all men.

PREFACE

It makes the story of his life significant far beyond the circle of those who knew him personally, and loved him, and love him still. He did, simply and directly, what every man can do if he will. In the simple practice of good-will, all men meet on common ground—the great and the small, the rich and the poor, the clever men and the men of smaller talents. If he had never become a great producer and merchant; if he had never made a dollar; if his name had never gone beyond those who knew him personally; his life still would have had this influence and proved this truth—that the power of individual good-will is the greatest power given to mankind.

Henry J. Heinz
A Biography

I
THE AMERICA OF HIS BOYHOOD

In 1844, when Henry J. Heinz was born in Birmingham (now the South Side of Pittsburgh), there was little or nothing to prophesy of the region as it is now. The population was meager and lived frugally, with agriculture as the basic occupation. No man dreamed of the Pittsburgh of today. No visions of fortune were dangled before the young generation. The only road to prosperity known by the people was the slow, steady one of earning and saving. The conditions of life laid upon all men the necessity for thrift, industry and patience. Self-reliance was bred in them, because the individual had to do for himself countless little and large things that an elaborate social and industrial machinery does for him today.

THE AMERICA OF HIS BOYHOOD

But there was one fact common to life in that time as it is to this. Work was drudgery or the reverse, according to the spirit with which it was accepted and done.

Young Heinz was one of those who did not make drudgery of it. Although he had to begin at the age of eight years to do a share of the family's labors, and though each year brought increasing duties, he never indicated in his reminiscent moods that his boyhood was anything but happy. He worked daily in his mother's kitchen garden. When it expanded, he sold its spare produce by going through the village with a basket. When he was ten years old, his industrial progress was marked by a wheelbarrow to displace the basket. Two years later his business had assumed the dignity of a horse and wagon. Thus, by the time he was twelve years old, circumstances already had set his foot on the path that was to lead him to a great success, though neither he nor his parents had such dreams.

They had a creed for him better than dreams. It was a creed of willingness—of willing self-denial, of willing sacrifice for others, of willing integrity. They did not have to preach it to their children in many words, for they lived it every day through all their lives. To the day of his death, Henry J. Heinz never ceased to honor them. He was fifty-five years old when his mother died, and his words about her were: "In living for the Master and serving Him, some things have been incalculably helpful, and I turn, especially at this time, with grateful heart to the teachings of my mother, whom only a week ago the Lord soothed to sleep. Many of her sayings ever stand guard around my thoughts or influence my actions." Again in the opening paragraph of his will, after declaring his faith in Christ and testifying how God had sustained him through a long life, he added: "This legacy was left me by my consecrated mother, who was a woman of strong faith, and to it I attribute any success I may have attained during my life."

Both his parents were born in Germany. His father's family had lived hundreds of years in the village of Kallstadt, Province of the Rheinpfalz, Bavaria, where the records showed generations, mostly vineyard-

THE AMERICA OF HIS BOYHOOD

owners, going back to 1608. His father was twenty-nine years old when he left Europe in 1840, for America, settling in Birmingham. Henry J. Heinz' mother, Anna Margaretta Schmidt, was born in Kruspis, a village near Hersfeld, Germany, where her father was burgomaster, and where her ancestors, too, had lived generation after generation. She accompanied relatives to America in 1843, and they, also, settled in Birmingham.

On December 4, 1843, they were married, and on October 11, 1844, their first child, Henry J. Heinz, was born. In 1849, when he was five years old, the family, enlarged by two other children, moved to Sharpsburg, six miles up the Allegheny, east of Pittsburgh. It was only a village, and in many respects villages in that region still had the characteristics of frontier settlements. The Great West was an unknown domain of prairies, buffalo herds and painted warriors who forbade entrance to the white man on pain of death. The first locomotive to be built in America had been turned out only nineteen years before—"The Best Friend,"

THE AMERICA OF HIS BOYHOOD

built in the foundry at West Point. Morse had invented his telegraph only nine years before Henry was born. Post offices were few. Most of the communication between large cities was by stage over post roads that were generally poor, and often frightful. The country roads were roads only in name. Corduroy and mud would make about the best description of them. Bottomless in spring and in the autumn rains, gashed and rutted in dry weather, they made any protracted journey an adventure calling for great exertion by men and animals.

Even a village like Sharpsburg, so near to Pittsburgh, was isolated and self-dependent to a degree almost incredible to men of this age. Undertakings that in this day are only ordinary, routine acts, often involved heavy labors and, sometimes, risk of life. Thus, when Henry J. Heinz was only a small fellow, who today might hardly be trusted to go far on city streets without an older companion, he was engaged by Pennington Ray, a friend of the family, to help him in moving from Freeport to Sharpsburg. It was only 23 miles; but the task called for a canal boat, which had to be towed by horses from Sharpsburg to Freeport and then back with the load.

On the way up, the tow-horse on which the boy was riding became entangled with the tow-line of a heavy and swift mule-drawn canal "packet" bound the other way. He slid from his horse just in time. The animal was jerked from the bank into the canal and under the passing boat. On the return trip, after a raw, snowy November day, he slipped on the deck and had an icy ducking for himself. An hour later it was his turn to drive the horses. The night was wild with cold rain and wind. The boat was frozen in finally, and he got such sleep as he could. His wet clothing was frozen stiff in the morning. He thawed it out as well as he could, and then drove the horses the rest of the way to Sharpsburg, where he arrived with face, hands and feet almost frozen.

These conditions of life made a rough school, and an effective one. It taught men to use not only their hands, but their heads, and to do it quickly, for errors of judgment brought swift, and often fatal, punishment.

THE AMERICA OF HIS BOYHOOD

The experiences of that life contributed much to his power of leadership in after years. He was able to direct how things should be done, because he himself knew how to do them. He was willing, too, at any moment to do them. His associates never were surprised when their president failed to appear at his office. They had learned to take it for granted that he was somewhere in the plant or the grounds with his coat off, working among the men to get at a better way of doing some task.

He delighted in such incidents; and his personal satisfaction in his own skin and knowledge was much the lesser part of his pleasure. His great satisfaction was that he had succeeded in passing on a new idea, or in promoting a new method, that would make for the greater comfort of men as well as for efficiency.

He was a tireless teacher, and his teaching sank in and took hold because it was wholly free from the sting of criticism. He taught not because he wanted to display superiority, but because he was a giver. When he discovered something useful, he could not rest till he had shared the discovery with others who might benefit. Whatever he knew he wanted to pass on.

His method was such that men hardly realized that he was teaching them. Thus, one day when lumber was being lifted to the upper story of a building in the plant, he saw that poor management was causing each man a maximum of hard labor, while with better direction one-half the number could do the work with more ease. Instead of ordering the change to be made, he laid aside his hat and coat and climbed to the top of the carload as if for a joke. It amused the men to see "the boss" take hold; and they acceded with immense good-will when he suggested after a few minutes: "Do you think we might make it easier by handling the stuff this way?" After a while he suggested a further improvement. Finally he mounted to the factory window, and began to take the lumber in, demonstrating without a word how one man at that post could do more with less exertion than it was then causing two. When he went away, the car was being unloaded as he had intended it should be; but not one

THE AMERICA OF HIS BOYHOOD

of the men had any humiliated sense of having been corrected.

It was help, not correction, that inspired his constant and eager teachership. He was always a student himself, and he took it for granted that others were as zealous to learn as he was. He did not want men to recognize that their improvement was due to his guidance. He often chuckled when somebody, whom he had led on, proudly called his attention to a new method, firm in the belief that he had originated it himself. In fact, he went to quite extraordinary trouble to make men believe that they themselves were suggesting or discovering what he wanted them to learn.

It was this kind of teaching that made the unique human organization which remains vital today, so inspired by his spirit that it is as if he were present in the body. He shared everything that he knew. He shared it with strangers on the street as well as with his own employees, from the farthest nooks of the plant to the board room where he met his fellow directors. They recall him today in terms of what they learned from him. Many times they ask, in face of a new problem:

THE AMERICA OF HIS BOYHOOD

"What would Mr. Heinz do?" They remember his practice of taking somebody with him whenever he had something important to develop, so that the new knowledge should be shared.

It was his faculty of teaching that enabled him to build up his huge organization almost entirely from within. He adhered to that principle from the beginning, and remained unshaken even during the era when nearly all American business men believed that the brilliant results could be gained only by the opposite course of hiring stars. While they were competing hotly for outside talent, Henry J. Heinz stuck to his own men, and promoted his own men. He never hired stars. He developed his own people, first, because they were his people, and, second, because he believed in what the world called "ordinary men." With the untiring patience, tact and thoughtfulness which are possible only to good-will, he proved that ordinary men have it in them to do many common things better than they have been done before, and to do many uncommon things too. There are men throughout the world today representing

THE AMERICA OF HIS BOYHOOD

the company in many ways and with brilliant success who started under him as boys. A man who drove a pair of mules for him when he began business was in charge of the whole huge system of warehousing and shipping that spreads a web over the entire country, before Mr. Heinz died. How his teaching stuck is pointed by an amusing little anecdote. Some years after his death a man in the incinerating department of the plant was instructed to change his methods in some minor detail. He sent back the firm answer: "I do this the way Mr. Heinz told me."

The Mother of Henry J. Heinz

II
LESSONS OF HOME

IT was the hope of his parents that their first born should enter the ministry. They were of that quietly devout European stock which, without bigotry or intolerance, handed down from generation to generation the conviction that the Bible was the supreme guide for all things, earthly as well as spiritual. It was a simple creed, but not narrow, for high in it stood charity. Margaretta Heinz taught her son a rule which he never forgot, and which he practiced so constantly that it became one of those traits for which men most loved him. It was: "Always remember to place yourself in the other person's shoes." His father so recognized the duties of neighborliness that it is remembered of him that he unhitched his team from his own plow to lend it to a neighbor whose need was pressing.

Of these parents, he said after the lapse of sixty years: "I had an honest father, and a mother with a Christlike spirit, in whom I had wonderful faith. She could handle me because she knew how to inspire me; because she knew what to say, when and how. I live under the spell of her many sayings." There is a card on the walls of the plant today, put up by Mr. Heinz, with the legend: "Not so much what you say, but how, when and where."

They sent him to school under the pastor of the Lutheran Church. Such a form of education was that of many village-trained boys of that time when schools and school teachers were not abundant. It fell naturally to the minister, as an educated man, to look after secular education in a small community, as well as spiritual instruction. The elder Heinz was treasurer of the school, which was in the village of Etna, one and one-half miles away. These school opportunities would be regarded today as most meager, as in fact they were. But it was the best that many country boys throughout North America of the fifties were getting, and it was better than many thousands of others received. Its limitations were in the variety and volume of imparted knowledge, rather than in the quality. It made only a foundation. But it was a sound foundation,

LESSONS OF HOME

adequate for any superstructure of learning that might be erected later.

To the father and mother at home, education was sacred, and they implanted in their son another trait that became an integral part of his character—a literally insatiable desire for knowledge. All through life he wanted to know. His temperament impelled him to seek information from men and from tangible sources rather than from books. He wanted to know at first hand. He used books to round out what he had learned.

He applied the method to all his pursuits —to art and science, to business, to public affairs. His associates in his own business and on the many boards and committees on which he served, often marveled at the extraordinary precision with which he forecast business conditions and other events of the future. He was, it is true, gifted with astonishing foresight. But the basis of his judgment and of his acts was the firm basis of knowledge. He had gone out and learned the facts—and when he went out to gather facts, he gathered them without letting his own opinions obtrude, and he acted on them

LESSONS OF HOME

without letting his previous opinions sway him. Very few men—amazingly few—possess this fundamental, vital principle of all learning—the principle of recognizing facts whole-heartedly even when they are exceedingly uncomfortable and unwelcome. It requires a mind of absolute integrity. To recognize truths, a man must love truth.

To him, truth was not just a pretty virtue to be admired. He considered truth to be as vital to a man as his vital organs. Tolerant himself, he tried to be tolerant even to liars; but it was quite impossible for him to view a liar as anything but a moral suicide.

One day he accosted a new employee at the weigher's platform weighing apples. The young man, eager to impress his value on his employer, said: "We are getting you good weight today, Mr. Heinz." "Fine!" said Mr. Heinz. "What are you doing for me?" "Why, you know, a quick eye, a quick hand, and you can always slip over a few pounds extra." Mr. Heinz nodded and after a moment asked him mildly to go with him to the office. When they arrived, he said: "Do you know what office this is? It's the cashier's office.

LESSONS OF HOME

You will be paid off, and you will leave this place at once."

"But, Mr. Heinz!" cried the astonished young man. "I was saving you money!"

"You were robbing a man who was selling to me," said Mr. Heinz, "and you were robbing me of something more precious." Then, laying his hand on the discharged man's shoulder, he added: "There is only one way to weigh, or to do anything else. Be as square to the other fellow as to yourself."

He was a square weigher in all things. It was one of his secrets of learning. He weighed facts and evidence squarely. In a presidential campaign many years ago, when he was on an important committee of his party, all his fellow members were convinced that victory for their side was a foregone conclusion, and their belief seemed amply sustained by all the news. He believed it himself—but he did not *know*. So he went out to learn. He sat down and chatted with bricklayers eating their midday meal on the street. He chatted with others. He did not debate. He asked men what they thought, and because he asked them simply and frankly, they gave him simple and frank answers. He returned and warned his committee that the party was in danger of defeat. They laughed at him. He went again into the highways and byways and gathered more facts for his note-book.

That note-book was not popular with his associates. They declined to assimilate the unpalatable memoranda of his talks. Afterward, when the party was defeated, they said that Henry J. Heinz had made a wonderfully good guess, or, if they were more polite, they credited him with wonderful political acumen. What he had done was simply what he always did. He had gone out to learn, and when he had learned, he weighed the facts squarely, though the scale-beam tipped in a way he did not welcome.

His note-book was a constant companion. He had an excellent memory, far superior to that of most men; but he made sure of everything that he wanted to preserve, by setting it down. Sooner or later there would arrive an occasion when a memorandum, sometimes made many years before, would be brought forth, to bear exactly on the issue.

Another companion was a tape measure. It became a half-humorous, half-serious habit of his traveling companions to provide themselves similarly, for nobody could tell at what moment it would be required—to measure the height of a door, the dimensions of a panel, the proportions that made some object beautiful. He was a builder—a builder of organization, a builder of principles, a builder of men; and in the actual field of building construction he gave the impulse its direct expression. He studied architecture as he studied everything that he undertook. Every journey was a university course for him.

As a collector of art, he learned as he collected, and he grew with his collections. When he began to collect antique watches, he knew nothing of the field. He began by buying a single watch of a specific period, without any great value either intrinsically or from the collector's point of view. He was paying to learn. He took that watch home and made a study of it. Then he turned to books and learned what specialists had to say about its period. So, piece by piece, he

LESSONS OF HOME

learned as he collected, until in the end he possessed many envied prizes and ranked as an expert.

His famous collection of carved ivories was made in the same way. To him it would have been utterly meaningless simply to hire other men's eyes and knowledge to acquire these exquisite things for him. Every piece represented his own patiently acquired knowledge and understanding. He did not pretend to be an artist, and he did not deceive himself or others by claiming that he had the artist's native ability for spontaneous perception of what was best. But he loved beauty with true reverence; and with the same simple, straightforward spirit with which he set himself to learn other things, he set himself to understand this great thing, and to understand it so that he might impart it to others for their pleasure and inspiration.

III
THE DIGNITY OF LABOR

MARGARETTA HEINZ, his mother, understood and delighted in the growing things of earth. She had sufficient household cares, but she always found time to sow and plant. The house in Sharpsburg soon had a bountiful kitchen garden, and its yield became more welcome year by year, for the family increased till there were eight children. It devolved on Henry, as the eldest, to help in the gardening, and he became imbued with his mother's ardor. So without intending it, she directed his course of life away from the ministry.

By the time he was twelve years old the garden covered three and one-half acres, and he was already doing a tidy little business in marketing the spare produce. His father, who was in the business of brick-making, had bought the land, but left its management entirely to his wife and son. When he was thirteen, he was confirmed in the Lutheran Church in Etna, and as confirmation then was equivalent to graduation, his further education came from what he got at home and from what he gave himself. By this time, however, his practical turn of mind and his bent for business had become so evident that his parents wisely yielded their preference for a church career, and allowed him to take the course that his impulse and his ability indicated.

Thus, a business genius was saved to the world, and the work of the ministry did not suffer. By collaboration, he did more for the church than he might have done by direct service within it. As a layman he gave it the best he had of heart and brain and means. For all preachers, he had an open door, plentiful time, and usually a generous gift. He liked their company and their talk. He suggested texts and sermons. His warmest interest was always with the struggling preacher and the humble church, and he did not permit his assistance to be circumscribed by limitations as to creed or doctrine. He believed that Heaven was high and wide enough to cover many theological differences.

His genius for business was not the "genius" that directs itself to making money

THE DIGNITY OF LABOR

without earning it. It was not even the kind that calculated too closely to make sure that a given expenditure of time and labor was not too great for the amount earned. Thus, when their own garden temporarily gave him a little spare time, he picked up potatoes for a neighboring farmer, a Mr. Cook, for a wage of twenty-five cents a day and board. This man Cook knew the stimulus of a special reward, so while Henry was piling up wealth at the rate of twenty-five cents daily, he offered three prizes to those who picked up the most potatoes: twenty-five cents, twelve and one-half cents and six and one-quarter cents. There were twenty contestants in the field, of whom Henry was the youngest. He made a good fight, but he was outclassed by the foreman, who won the first prize, and by a lad of eighteen who won the second. However, he came in third; and he was so proud that he carried home the six and one-quarter cents—a "fi-penny-bit," as it was called—that he remembered it and told of it more than a half a century afterward.

He had to learn to do a little of everything. The Allegheny River, unruly then as

THE DIGNITY OF LABOR

now, often disported itself at high-water seasons by washing away a part of the family garden. A family council decided that the only way to protect it definitely was to defend it with gravel piled deep and massive enough to make an embankment. Henry's father supplied an old horse, "Baldy," and a scraper. With these the boy, by himself, drew the great quantities of heavy gravel from the lower reach of the river and piled it up along the frontage of the property.

With it all, he managed to find time to lend a hand in his father's brick-yard. At first he "off bore" brick, and did other tasks of purely manual labor. Later, after he had taken a course in Duff's Business College in Pittsburgh, he utilized his knowledge of bookkeeping to keep the accounts. He came to know as much about brick as he knew about horse-radish roots and other parts of his work; and when anybody asked him in after years how he had found time to do so much, he liked to repeat John Wanamaker's reply to a similar question: "Oh, we country boys work!"

THE DIGNITY OF LABOR

Although he did not remain in the brick business, he found amply profitable use for his knowledge of brick in his later years, just as he found abundant and profitable use for his early knowledge of horses. His many building operations were successful because he had not only made brick but had learned how brick should be erected. The pleasing and apparently time-defying exteriors of the main plant buildings in Pittsburgh are due largely to his own skill in building and to his personal selection of all the brick used. A good job of brick-making or of bricklaying never escaped his eye. If he saw particularly fine brick anywhere, even in a distant city, samples of it would be sure to arrive in Pittsburgh by express. One of his associates said that according to his observation the chief use Mr. Heinz made of his office desk was for stowage of sample brick.

It was the same way with horses. Almost all the horses used by the Heinz institution in all its branches and activities throughout the United States were bought by himself. He liked the task too much to delegate it to others. For the horses to draw the company wagons, he selected animals of uniform weight and type. He initiated the idea, never since violated, that every Heinz horse everywhere was to be of pure black color; and before the introduction of automobiles Heinz teams and wagons in every city were the same —the wagons enameled white with green trimmings, and the horses black. They were good horses, too. Among the horse-breeders and horse-traders of the country, he had the reputation of being as good a horse-buyer as there was. He knew when a horse was good, and he knew what it was worth. One day when a dealer sent him word that he had a fine four-hundred-dollar horse for two hundred dollars, Mr. Heinz sent back the message that when he had a four-hundred-dollar horse for four hundred dollars, he would be glad to see it.

He was able to handle almost any horse, and he remained a horseman until the roads were so monopolized by the automobile that even he could not risk animals on them longer. His skill with the reins, and his serene confidence in what he could do with a horse, were such that many a man whom he took

THE DIGNITY OF LABOR

driving for the first time was equally relieved and astonished at getting off with a whole skin. Those who knew Mr. Heinz better knew that his apparently venturesome driving was not reckless. He was fearless with a horse as he was with anything else that he understood; but he never gave a horse or an enterprise the chance to run beyond his control.

One of his fine horses was the famous "Nightshade," which, retired on a pension of abundant oats, hay and green pasture, reached the venerable age of twenty-three and died only a few days before his old master. Long after he had ceased to use him, he went to look after him. He never forgot any of his horses. He never forgot even old "Baldy," which had hauled the scraper when he was a little lad.

As his early labors had given him mastery over horses, so had they given him a body of sound health and a muscular strength that was concealed by his apparently slight figure. Among other attributes not usually suspected in a business man were wrists of quite unusual power, which were acquisitions from

THE DIGNITY OF LABOR

his boyhood work in the brick-yard. When he saw men handling brick, it was always easy for him to judge what they were accomplishing. In one case, as he walked along the street at his Pittsburgh factory, he saw a particularly husky chap to whom the others were pitching one brick at a time. There was a smile when, after asking if he might take a hand, he laid aside his high-crowned hat, his trim coat and his cane. He began by pitching one brick at a time slowly, then faster and faster until his man evinced every sign of being as busy as he wanted to be. Then he suddenly began to pitch two bricks at a time. "Hey!" shouted the man. "What are you trying to do?" "Why," said Mr. Heinz, pitching faster, "we used to pitch them four at a time. Look out!" and he sent in three at a time. When he walked off, the crowd that had gathered to watch gave him the cheers due to championship form. He used to say with a twinkle in his eye: "When I went away, they were no longer pitching one brick at a time."

If his abiding pleasure in physical work had been simply due to pride in his own

THE DIGNITY OF LABOR

personal fitness, these anecdotes would have little significance. Their deeper value is due to the fact that respect for labor permeated his whole character. "The dignity of labor" was a vital fact for him. It was one of the greatest realities of his life, and respect for the laboring man was a spontaneous attitude that ruled all his relations and dealings with men. When he spoke to the most obscure worker, performing the most humble of duties, his words and manner were not dictated by policy. They were genuine; and in this lies perhaps the most important secret for industrial relations. Men will appreciate justice and fair dealing even when they are dictated only by policy; but in that case the feeling of appreciation is only mental. It does not, and can not, go deeper. Every man, no matter what his caliber may be, can "sense" good-will or the lack of it. It can not be simulated. It has to be there, and if it is there, its simple, straightforward power is worth all the policies that ever were invented or ever will be.

Mr. Heinz was always willing to put himself into the other man's shoes, and he was

THE DIGNITY OF LABOR

able to do it because he had learned. He never looked back on his own manual labor in youth with any feeling that it represented an inferior stage of his life, and he did not even look back upon it as a stage that he had escaped from, and that was over and done with. It was ever present in his thoughts, like the keystone of an arch. It followed naturally and inevitably that he thought of his employees and of himself in common terms. He always spoke and thought of the Heinz establishment as a union—"a union," as he liked to put it, "of employer and employee, one in heart and effort."

It is recalled that at one time when a new building was being erected in the plant, a committee delegated from a building union called on him to demand that the work be done by union labor. "I am glad to see you," he said. "Now say just what you think, and I'll say just what I think. We ought to know each other, and we ought to understand each other." When they intimated that they would call a strike if their demands were not met, he stopped them with a smile. "I don't think we ought to threaten each other," he said.

THE DIGNITY OF LABOR

"That would be only a quarrel, not a discussion. I know that there are many good reasons why men feel that they must organize. So let us talk it over with mutual good-will."

After he had heard them out, he said: "All right. I'll accept your point of view on this job. It's a contractors' job, and you can go to them and tell them that we have agreed to make it a union job. Now I want you to do something for me. We have a union in our own place here. We think it's the best kind of a union—a union of employer and employees. I'm going to ask you to go through our plant. Investigate it all you please. Talk to whomever you please. Ask them anything you please. And then—if you don't find anything to criticize in our relations, if you can't find that things would be better if the plant were unionized in your way, I am going to ask you to leave us alone here to work out our industrial relations as we are trying to do."

The delegates took him at his word. They went into every nook and corner. When they returned to the office, the spokesman said:

THE DIGNITY OF LABOR

"Mr. Heinz, we have had a regular education in what might be done in every industry. Our hands are off."

It is obvious that this was good, though bold, tactics. What won the delegates, however, was something bigger than tactics. They realized that Mr. Heinz was taking them at their face value, that he was willing to trust to their fairness. This, also, was one of his inborn traits. He was never afraid to trust a man. He always assumed that a man was honest and meant to do the right thing.

It happened one time that a carload of supplies from a shipper of whom Mr. Heinz bought a carload a week was reported as showing a short pack in every barrel. He had various barrels opened and examined them himself. "Put this whole carload into the cellars," he said, "and hold it there till you hear from me." He shook his head when his buyer wanted to complain to the consignor. "No," he said. "Just wait." He simply refrained from sending the next order, with the natural result that the shipper telegraphed anxiously. Mr. Heinz wrote back saying that any time he was in Pittsburgh

THE DIGNITY OF LABOR

he might drop in. The shipper arrived on the first train, and Mr. Heinz took him to the storage place, and ordered the barrels to be brought forward and opened. "Why, Mr. Heinz," exclaimed the man, "these barrels aren't full! They've been packed dead wrong." Mr. Heinz laughed and tapped him on the shoulder. "Remember you said that, and not I," he remarked. "I felt sure you wouldn't pack goods that way, but I wanted you to see just what had happened, so that you could correct your employees."

"Mr. Heinz," said the shipper, "I will never forget being treated this way; all I can say is, that as long as I live you will get my best quality and at a lower price than I quote to anybody else."

In his impulse for saving other men's feelings, he often, in fact habitually, went to what many business men might consider unnecessary trouble. But he never subscribed to the tenet that business has no time to consider feelings. Part of the strength of his organization was in the fact that men's errors, and even their transgressions, were not dealt with in a "businesslike" manner,

THE DIGNITY OF LABOR

but in the spirit of friendship and mutual regard. It was another expression of his respect for others, and another application of his mother's teaching about putting himself into the other person's shoes.

This practice, which he built into the very structure of the business founded by him, did not encourage laxness, but, indeed, accomplished the exact reverse. The intense regard for precision and thoroughness in all the innumerous little things of business, to which he trained his whole organization, remains the creed of the business today as if he still were present in body, because every individual knew that he could afford to admit a mistake, as there was no danger of humiliating rebuke. In fact, Mr. Heinz might almost be said to believe in mistakes, so warm was his sympathy for the person who acknowledged one frankly. His way of getting at it usually was: "Now, how would it be if we tried it this way?"

He made it understood that he considered every man entitled to one mistake of a kind. It was the same mistake a second time that he objected to. He went so far as to offer a

THE DIGNITY OF LABOR

prize for the man who caught himself in the most mistakes in a given period, and had the courage to set them down and read the record publicly. The plan was a great success. The most denunciatory criticism from the most ironlike disciplinarian could not have made such an educational and disciplinary session as was held when employee after employee stood up and told on himself. And the lesson was all the better learned because of the fact that nobody felt hurt, but that it was a lesson given in the spirit of good humor.

One of his associates, who is an officer and director in the company today, started in with him as a boy. When he was earning $45 a month he made an error that caused a loss of $76. Instead of charging him with it, Mr. Heinz led him to discover and report it himself, and then led him on to acknowledge the seriousness of the mistake and to volunteer to pay for it. "Very well," said Mr. Heinz. "I think you should," and they agreed on a deduction of $5 a month from his salary. When pay day arrived, the cashier handed him $45 as usual. "You've forgotten

THE DIGNITY OF LABOR

to take out that $5," said the lad. "Oh, no," replied the cashier. "We have deducted it all right, and you are going to keep on having it deducted, all right, till you pay it up. But, you see, Mr. Heinz told us to raise your salary $5 a month."

Nobody ever made the mistake of thinking that these traits meant softness of will—or, at least, nobody made such a mistake more than once. He was a man of intense convictions and intense will power, and when at the proper time he unleashed his forces, there were few men who cared to try conclusions with him. One of those who did try it, said ruefully afterward: "Say, tell me! How is it that the old man can kick the gizzard out of a man, and then, if he jumped into the river, we'd all jump in after him?"

IV
EARLY BUSINESS VENTURES

IN his boyhood it had not occurred to men that the pursuit of the merchant might be made a branch of scientific public education. The America of his day was not blessed with any such literature as we have today, dealing with business and business principles. A few "business colleges" here and there represented the only attempt at tuition, and their chief idea was that business education meant a course in bookkeeping. The majority of business men would have smiled ironically at the idea of a business training that involved academic study of basic theories and principles. The prevailing idea was that it had to be learned by rule of thumb; and if men did not actually assert that it was largely a matter of hit-and-miss, most of them assuredly conducted it on that basis.

To a certain extent this attitude was almost natural. Never before in history had mankind known such a gigantic reservoir of natural wealth, all lying before every man's eyes, and most of it free to every man who

EARLY BUSINESS VENTURES

had the instinct of exploitation. The vast adventure of tearing open a whole rich continent could hardly do otherwise than to breed impatience with anything that did not savor of impetuous, headlong action. "Yesterday" and "Tomorrow" were conceptions to which the eager young America was equally indifferent.

It was inevitable that business men should have thought that ethics of business, as we know them today, were visionary. Business failures and bank suspensions were daily commonplaces, over which people got excited only in those periodic intervals when they assumed catastrophic proportions. In that confused time, the first daily business of every man, as he saw it, was to look after his own skin.

Young Henry, ambitious, and eagerly bent on going ahead, might have accepted these methods and made them his own. If the dog-eat-dog policy was not actually honored in his time, there was at any rate small pity for the one who allowed himself to be eaten. If he had hung his neighbors' hides on his fence, he would have incurred

EARLY BUSINESS VENTURES

no odium. The phrase of the day, "a smart business man," was a cloak that covered many sins.

But there was no temptation to him in success gained on such terms. He knew the value of money, and he knew the need for money. But even in his boyhood, when he saved every penny, money was not the first consideration with him. His parents had taught him thrift, but not greed. They knew nothing of get-rich-quick business. All that they knew was to have horror of ill-gotten gain; to desire nothing unless it had been fairly earned; to refuse any advantage that meant hurt to any person; and to prefer honor and a good name to any other success.

These principles were part of the boy's very blood. They made him sound. He founded his business career on these principles from the beginning, because anything else was impossible to him. They were as much part of him as his head and hands. Years after his vegetable-selling days had passed, an old grocer said: "I used to like to buy from Henry. I always paid him a little more than I paid anybody else, but what he sold me was not only more satisfactory on the average, but I never lost money on what I bought from him."

He looked out for his customers in that early day because it was natural for him to do it. Without knowing it, he was building business on a basis years ahead of his time. He was shaping personal principles and moral principles into the corner-stones of business policy that today, more than half a century later, are the acknowledged foundations for all business.

Reviewing his career when this book was going to press, one who was close to him said: "There is one thing in which he was fortunate beyond most human beings. I think that even in boyhood, he had little of the ordinary human weakness in the face of temptations. In all the years I knew him, I cannot recall anything—pleasure, money, comfort or fame—that ever tempted him to step an inch from his steady path. And I think it one of the fine proofs of his humanness that, though temptation meant so little to him, he still understood others who were

EARLY BUSINESS VENTURES

tempted, and met them with sympathy and compassion."

When he was sixteen, the garden had so grown that he employed three or four women and developed a market for three deliveries a week to Pittsburgh grocers. It was the general custom to deliver fresh produce in Pittsburgh between four and five o'clock in the morning. The farmers had to pick the stuff the night before and load it, so they could start for market in the small hours of the morning.

Henry conformed to the custom for a time, but he could see no sense in it. He wasn't afraid to get up at three o'clock in the morning, as he had to, but he failed to see why there should be so much waste motion with no result except to wake up all the grocers in Pittsburgh hours before their day's sales could begin. When he had thought it out, he showed his customers that they got the same vegetables that they might have the night before, and he proposed to save them early rising by making his deliveries between eight and nine o'clock at night. They had never heard of such a thing, but he convinced

EARLY BUSINESS VENTURES

them that it was for their own comfort, and he succeeded in bringing about his first revolution in method.

His next thought was in the direction of specialized service, and his first effort was with one of the family crops—horse-radish. At that time, people bought their horse-radish in the form of the roots in the market, and grated them for themselves. It was anything but pleasant work. Many have been the tears shed in the process, as the experienced well know. The young gardener undertook to save the housewife both the labor and the tears, by grating and bottling the product and selling it in package form ready for use. It was the germ from which the business of H. J. Heinz Company as a packer of food products developed. A few years later he wrote out a long memorandum —several thousand words—describing the cultivation and care of horse-radish roots, trimming and storing, grating and bottling. He noted on it that it was "for the benefit of the younger men who may succeed me in that which has cost much labor and toil."

EARLY BUSINESS VENTURES

He had not, however, yet arrived at the point of concentrating all his efforts on food products. He was taking more and more part in his father's business of brick-making, and other business opportunities always found him ready. Apparently there never was a time, even in his early youth, when idleness had attractions, and he never changed in this respect. He knew how to rest, but rest meant change of occupation, not non-occupation. He selected occupations that represented play to him—art collection, building, public service, travel.

Among various early ventures was a winter's experience in the ice business. Ice was selling at five cents a pound, and was in good demand in Oil City, and his father entered into partnership with Pennington Ray to cut and store ice on Hemlock Creek, about fourteen miles above the town. Henry, then nineteen, looked after the business in Oil City.

Unluckily for them, two factors entered —over-production and over-competition. Jack Frost, in collaboration with Hemlock Creek and all other rivers and creeks in

EARLY BUSINESS VENTURES

Pennsylvania, produced an enormous ice crop. Everybody cut ice and tried to sell it. Ice dropped to one cent a pound, and the profits of the ice business evaporated. The partnership was dissolved, and it fell to Henry to drive four horses and an empty ice wagon back to Sharpsburg, some eighty miles from Oil City.

In later years Mr. Heinz often told of that trip with the empty wagon, not because it was important in itself, but because it pointed his never-ending battle against waste. There was no man who more hated waste of any kind—waste of material, waste of time, waste of human opportunity. He could, and did, treat with equanimity and patience, losses large and small that were due to error or lack of judgment or other such human faults. But the hatred of waste was so ingrained in him that he often puzzled less careful men by pausing in most important work to investigate and eliminate some petty waste.

To drive an empty wagon eighty miles was a waste that annoyed young Henry just as it would have annoyed the older and

EARLY BUSINESS VENTURES

richer Henry. He couldn't find a remedy before he left Oil City, and he didn't find one during the first part of the trip. But he had it before he reached the town of Butler, forty miles from Pittsburgh. He went to a produce merchant and said: "I have no money, but I have an empty wagon that I'm driving through to Sharpsburg. If you will furnish goods to carry, I will sell them at my destination and account for the proceeds."

Perhaps he won the day by gaining the merchant's faith in his integrity, rather than by the commercial soundness of his proposition, sound and sensible though it was. He got a lot of butter, eggs and oats which he sold, leaving the money with a merchant in Etna who was known to both parties to the bargain. He delivered his empty ice wagon at Sharpsburg with a profit of twenty-five dollars to pay for the trip. In after days, when instead of a single wagon he had to deal with his own railroad cars in whole trains, the very same spirit made it impossible for him to waste railroad mileage, but because in that case the savings were impressive in amount, and because they demanded foresight and often inventive genius, men were prone to forget that at the bottom of all these efficiencies was just that hatred of waste which he had learned in his boyhood.

By his constant fight against waste in little things he inculcated throughout his whole organization a habit of orderliness, precision and tidiness that became a really powerful and dominating factor in the production of quality. When he gave hours, as he often did, to the correction of an apparently trivial waste that did not seem to amount to more than a few pennies, he did it because he perceived that it had fundamental importance in the whole conduct of the plant. He always explained his reasons; and thus, the employees of the whole establishment learned to understand that their elimination of every small waste was not for reasons of pettiness or small economy, but that it had intimate bearing on the ability of the Heinz Company to discard unhesitatingly any quantity of raw material, however great, that did not measure up to the standard set for it.

EARLY BUSINESS VENTURES

He never figured his time by its money value. He figured its value wholly in terms of what he could accomplish with it, and this same trait was one that marked his youth. Thus, as he had done his share of the garden work without thinking of pay, he had done his share of work in the brick-making establishment without pay. However, when he reached twenty-one, his savings (which had been started with the wages he had earned as potato picker for the farmer, Cook, and the "fi-penny-bit" prize) amounted to enough to enable him to purchase a half interest in his father's brick business, and his father was glad to have him.

One of the first things that the new partner did was to install heating flues and drying apparatus that permitted brick manufacture to be done through the winter, where till then they had been made only in the summer. It was thus possible to accumulate stock for the spring, which was the season of active demand.

A year later another idea that had been incubating in his mind was brought to

EARLY BUSINESS VENTURES

reality. If men could make money by buying brick and building them into walls, why couldn't he build walls with his own brick and make money? He took contracts for the brickwork in several buildings, some of which still were standing years after his death to bear testimony to the quality of the brick and the character of the construction.

He learned that 750,000 bricks were required, at Flemming Station on the Ohio River below Pittsburgh, and he went after the contract and got it. It was a job independent of the Sharpsburg plant, and he had a profit of a thousand dollars to show for the six months which the making of the brick required. He turned another profit because, observing that the coal supply at Flemming Station was fluctuating and uncertain, he undertook to ship coal from Pittsburgh in barges.

In 1868, when he was twenty-four years old, he formed a partnership with L. C. Noble to manufacture brick at Beaver Falls, Pennsylvania. This was his first business activity outside of the family. Mr. Noble was to supervise the Beaver Falls plant with

The Home in Sharpsburg which Henry J. Heinz Built for His Father

EARLY BUSINESS VENTURES

occasional visits by the other partner, who continued to take an active part in the business with his father, who was also staying right by the horse-radish enterprise. He was an expansionist constitutionally. He could not be satisfied to stand still. His ideas always kept ahead of realization. At the same time they did not become visionary. He was enough of an idealist to furnish the motive for expanding programs. He was enough of a realist to anchor his ideals to solid earth.

When he was twenty-four, his love for building got its first concrete expression, and in a direction most natural to him, because it was a structure typifying the family loyalty. The elder Heinz had long wished to revisit Europe, and in 1868, with his business well established and safe under his son, he departed. Scarcely had he left, before his son started work on the surprise that he had planned to celebrate his home-coming—a new home, larger and more comfortable than the home which the family had occupied so many years, and which had become crowded as the eight children grew older. His experience as a contractor stood him

EARLY BUSINESS VENTURES

in good stead, for the new residence that he erected was surpassed by few houses in Sharpsburg at the time, and still stands as a good house.

When the father returned, the joy of the home-coming almost began to dissipate at the sight of the elaborate new house. "Oh, Henry, Henry!" he cried. "Why have you done this? We can't afford it. It will break me to pay for it." The laughing family crowded around him and told him that Henry had already paid for it, and that the money had come from the collection of old accounts which Heinz senior had long ago given up as worthless.

V
THE FIRST PARTNERSHIP

THE year 1869 was a notable year for him. He married, and he formed a firm which became the lineal ancestor to today's company. His marriage made him doubly fortunate, for his bride, Sarah Sloan Young, brought to his new household what his mother had given to him in the old—devotion, faith, and the understanding that knits a man's home and his career into unity, whole and complete. Like his mother, she had a serene courage in the face of trouble; and trouble was to come early in their married life, for the United States was approaching a period of business catastrophe which engulfed men far and wide.

The firm formed by Mr. Heinz was a partnership with his former partner in the brick business, L. C. Noble, a son of one of the chief families of Sharpsburg. The concern, under the name of Heinz and Noble, was formed to raise horse-radish and to bottle the grated product. Henry Heinz was twenty-five years old, and as he had begun

THE FIRST PARTNERSHIP

to learn the cultivation of vegetable products when he was eight, it may be said that this firm represented the first definite results of the patience and industry of seventeen years.

His ambitions had grown with the years, and the partnership was formed with great visions for the future. He did not, indeed, dream of such an institution as it was his fortune to build ultimately, but he had the absolute faith that a business in food products of unquestioned quality could be made into a big enterprise.

Despite this faith, and despite their ambitious hopes, they started on so small a scale that it might have seemed as if Henry J. Heinz, instead of having progressed in life, had sagged back to his original beginnings in boyhood. The firm's operations began with three-quarters of an acre cultivated for horse-radish, and the grating, bottling, warehousing and selling were conducted in one room and the basement of the house from which the family had only recently removed.

This practice of starting things on a small scale was one that he adhered to in after

THE FIRST PARTNERSHIP

years. It was not due to timidity or hesitancy. One of his marked characteristics was a courage that enabled him to undertake ventures which seemed almost reckless to men who did not know the exactness and completeness of the information on which he acted. But he was never satisfied to do anything until he knew all about it, and to his simple and direct manner of thought, the best way to find out was to try it experimentally. There was nothing timid or hesitating about these trials. They were as complete as they could be made. He adhered to the principle long after H. J. Heinz Company had reached a point where it could easily afford to venture directly on promising enterprises. If a new method of selling, a new idea in advertising or other similar changes were proposed and approved, he made a thorough test of them in one limited locality first.

It was this practice that had much to do with establishing each of his food products solidly in public esteem almost as soon as it was put on the market. He could not be induced to add a product to the Heinz list until

THE FIRST PARTNERSHIP

every conceivable trial had been made of it. As the demand for the original products grew, and brought with it a demand for additional varieties, a stranger at a meeting of the company's directors might have imagined at times that Mr. Heinz was strenuously opposed to the production of a new line. It might be that he himself had proposed its manufacture; but between that idea and the actual production and marketing of it, he interposed the most elaborate system of what might almost be called destructive research and criticism. He wanted his whole organization to hunt for the weak spots. He wanted his whole organization to know all that could be known about any given product before he would go further with it. He wanted to know that the necessary raw material could assuredly be procured in undiminishing quality, year after year. He wanted to know that his organization was able to make the product better than it was being made elsewhere.

After a new product had been completely approved as to quality and flavor, and its potential value as an addition to the list had

The First Desk used by Mr. Heinz in Sharpsburg, 1869

THE FIRST PARTNERSHIP

been satisfactorily established within the organization, as well as by trial in a selected circle outside, he still did not proceed to put it on the market. Having satisfied himself that it was good, he wanted to learn how it would strike the public. So he tried it out in one locality, often in only one town or city. He was always willing to assume that the public might not agree with him and his organization as to its desirability. He wanted to learn, and he did it with the same spirit that impelled him to chat with the workers on the streets to find out what people thought about public questions.

Once he was assured that his premises were sound, few men were likely to move more quickly or to go farther than he. He would suddenly, almost overnight, expand a small, cautious, local campaign into a sweeping one that covered the whole North American continent, or that might cover the world.

Usually his fellow directors were prepared for these quick decisions, and approved of them, no matter how great an undertaking they might involve, because he shared all his

THE FIRST PARTNERSHIP

ideas and thoughts with them, and kept them informed to the last detail. He had none of the vanity that induces many men to act as if their ideas were mysterious gifts vouchsafed only to unique minds.

Sometimes, however, his associates were likely to be startled by some unusually daring plan. At such times, he recognized openly that they were doing their duty; and if he could not convince them that his scheme was sound, he frequently got them to let him carry it through personally, with the understanding that he would bear the loss out of his own pocket if it failed.

The London factory was established under those conditions. He agreed with his fellow directors that it would require many years and large annual investments to make it pay. But he was sure that it would succeed, and they were not. Therefore, he insisted on making it his personal venture. But before long his directors insisted on taking their share, as they had learned to know that the things he was willing to pay for invariably succeeded. Today it is one of the largest and most profitable parts of the H. J. Heinz

THE FIRST PARTNERSHIP

Company business. He had been willing to pay for his mistake, if it were one, but he had taken pains by long personal investigation in Europe to avoid a mistake. A solid foundation for any enterprise always was the most important point in any undertaking.

The small beginning in 1869 meant a solid foundation of sound product. It meant that he had not undertaken more than he could handle at the start. It enabled him to put out the Heinz and Noble horse-radish with the personal knowledge that every bottle was as he wanted it to be. It was not long before the product had the kind of demand that he desired—a demand created by purchasers. When each day brought repeat orders, the young firm was confronted, of course, with the opportunity that has tempted and undone many producers—the opportunity to turn out a larger volume of product at the expense of the established quality. But this was no lure to Henry Heinz. Since boyhood, his whole life and character had shaped themselves, consciously and unconsciously, on the principle of moral

THE FIRST PARTNERSHIP

obligation that business today recognizes under the word "Service." In his day, men considered a transaction closed when they had delivered the tangible merchandise. He had been thinking farther ahead. The mere fulfillment of the letter of a contract was not enough for him. He wanted the consumer to get the worth of every penny that he paid, and he wanted the dealer to profit, not only in cash, but in holding a satisfied customer. So the firm of Heinz and Noble stuck to the plan of making only the amount of horseradish that they could make just as they wanted to make it; and they increased their output only as they managed to increase their capacity for making it that way.

In our time, every young beginner in business has learned that this is the only principle on which a permanent business can be founded. But in the period of half a century ago, only a very few men realized it, and fewer still had the steady patience to stick to it. In that half century tens of thousands of business enterprises had been launched, often on a great scale. All have vanished—all except those firms that today can point to a

THE FIRST PARTNERSHIP

consistent and unbroken practice of integrity in product.

It was not until 1871, two years after they had started, that they felt safe in enlarging. Then they took in some more rooms in the old house, rented a small building near by, and added two other prepared products to their line—celery sauce and pickles. A year later, in 1872, the business had so increased that a new partner, E. J. Noble, brother of L. C. Noble, was admitted to the firm, which assumed the title Heinz, Noble and Company. The new partner had a two-eighths interest, and each of the original partners held three-eighths. The horse-radish cultivation was increased until by 1874 the three-quarter acre patch had expanded to twenty-five acres, and, to obtain the other vegetables that they required, the firm was cultivating one hundred acres of fertile Allegheny River Valley land about a mile above Sharpsburg.

VI
A PERIOD OF TROUBLE

Every great soul has its crown fashioned in the furnace of suffering and sorrow. The lofty personalities of history, and the pioneers and prophets of the race, have been tried by fire; their characters have been perfected through suffering.

Four years after the founding of the partnership, a black storm swept the United States—a disaster which remains recorded in history as the Panic of 1873. It spread ruin far and wide, and equally great were the ills that followed it. For years afterward, its effects, direct and indirect, brought recurrent business troubles, many of which were, in fact, serious panics in themselves.

The young firm weathered the great panic, and continued to grow so soundly that in 1875 a leased location was taken on Second Avenue, Pittsburgh, and a branch distributing warehouse opened in St. Louis under the management of J. D. Graves, to be followed soon afterward with another branch house in Chicago.

A PERIOD OF TROUBLE

A new source of supply of vegetables became imperative. After careful survey of conditions, an arrangement was made with a canning and pickling company at Woodstock, Illinois, which desired an outlet for some six hundred acres of cultivated land. On January 20, 1875, Heinz, Noble and Company contracted to take the produce of the tract, at the rate of sixty cents a bushel for cucumbers and ten dollars a ton for cabbage. Under the agreement, L. C. Noble, representing the firm at Woodstock, was to issue checks, payable in Pittsburgh, as the crop came in from the fields, and Mr. Heinz, managing the plant and business in Pittsburgh, looked after the maintenance of the necessary bank funds. He had made careful provisions for the financing of an average size crop, and there was every reason to anticipate the best results from the venture.

But 1875 turned out to be a year of phenomenal crops. By the latter part of August, cucumbers were coming in from the fields at the rate of two thousand bushels a day, calling for twelve hundred dollars in daily payments for that crop alone, to say nothing of cabbage and other vegetables.

A PERIOD OF TROUBLE

Under normal conditions, Mr. Heinz, whose credit in Pittsburgh was excellent, could easily have borrowed the necessary additional funds from the banks to meet the demands of the bumper crop. But it happened that just then another serious financial disturbance passed over the land. Banks failed. Others could not honor the checks of their own depositors readily. The surviving financial institutions were so desperately put to it to remain solvent that they dared not lend a dollar, even on the best security or to the most respected borrower. Business houses, far older and more firmly established than Heinz, Noble and Company, were failing on every side.

Great as was his anxiety for the business that he had labored so hard to upbuild, his anxiety for the maintenance of his unspotted credit was by far the more intense of his worries. He wrote in his diary at the time:

> October 27—"I have, by the aid and strength of God, saved the firm's paper from protest."
> October 29—"I have been nearly crazed at times, protecting checks from Woodstock."

A PERIOD OF TROUBLE

November 2—"I have two thousand
    dollars to meet tomorrow, and not
    a penny to meet it with."

The huge crop continued to roll in. No power could stay it. For another month he succeeded, by unremitting effort, in meeting every day's demands. But on December 8 he had reached the end of all possible resources, and at the same time he succumbed at last to an illness which the strain and agony of the past months had produced. It was Friday, and Saturday was pay day at the plant. Before he went to bed, he met it by borrowing seven hundred dollars from his wife, who advanced it out of her own little bank account of seventeen hundred dollars that had been hers before marriage. He had not asked her before for a penny, but he asked her then; and it was not the least of his pain that he should have to do it.

She sustained him with bright courage that never flagged. Side by side with her in bravery stood his mother, who repeated her faith in him when he said to her from his sick-bed: "Mother, I fear we shall not be able to pull through the panic. You and

Mr. and Mrs. Henry J. Heinz on their Wedding Trip

A PERIOD OF TROUBLE

father have always inspired me with the thought that an honest man could not fail in business, but I am afraid that our firm will have to be numbered among the thousands that are failing daily. Father and you and other relatives have loaned me money which I have sent to our Western factory. Sallie loaned the firm seven hundred dollars yesterday to complete the pay-roll. I have just received a telegram that a seventeen-hundred-dollar check from Woodstock will reach the bank here Monday, and I am too sick to do anything more.

The crash came; but his manner of meeting his creditors was such that almost all felt good-will and confidence, and those who had been personal friends became still warmer and closer. His books showed that to the last moment he had striven to meet the firm's obligations. He had poured in everything that he owned. He had borrowed from his parents and others to save the credit of the concern. He was able to say to his creditors, as he did: "We gave up all for the benefit of our creditors. Many good men have gone down to failure in this panic."

A PERIOD OF TROUBLE

The Christmas that followed close upon the disaster was one that he never forgot. He, who so loved that season, who so loved to give that even in his poorest days he had managed to find little gifts for those dear to him, wrote in his diary: "No Christmas gifts to exchange. Sallie seemed grieved, and cried, yet said it was not about our troubles; only she did not feel well. It is grief. I wish no one such trials. I have no Christmas gifts to make."

But the family circle ringed him round, unshaken and true. In accordance with the family custom of gathering at the old home on Christmas Day, he and his family arrived at his mother's home. She gave him a Christmas gift—a printed card bearing these words:

> "May the blessings of thy God wait upon thee, and the sun of glory shine round thy head. May the gates of plenty, honor and happiness always open to thee and thine; may no strife disturb thy days, nor sorrow distress thy nights; may the pillow of peace kiss thy cheek, and the pleasures of imagination attend thy dreams; and when length of years makes thee tired of earthly joys, and the curtains of death gently close

A PERIOD OF TROUBLE

around the scenes of thine existence, may the angels of God attend thy bed and take care that the expiring lamp of life shall not receive one rude blast to hasten its extinction; and finally, may the Saviour's blood wash thee from all impurities and at last usher thee into the land of everlasting felicity."

He received it as a prophecy and a benediction. Grieved at the destruction of his hopes, and still more deeply grieved at the loss that had fallen on others, he faced a new future with courage undiminished. And as a first step he opened a little book of accounts which he marked with the inscription on the front cover:

M. O. BOOK OF HENRY J. HEINZ, 1875

signifying that it was a record of his moral obligations arising from the firm's failure. Although the legal discharge from bankruptcy meant a release from all the debts concerned in it, he entered the name of each creditor and the amount of his claim, and charged himself with the obligation of paying the amount due from himself personally as a partner with three-eighths interest in the concern.

A PERIOD OF TROUBLE

Many years after he had paid it all off, a friend came to him and said: "Mr. Heinz, the wagon builder, Mr.——is in sad trouble. The sheriff is to sell the furniture in his home tomorrow."

The man had been one of the few creditors who had shown hostility. He had made matters as difficult for Mr. Heinz as he could, and had indulged in bitter personal abuse in addition. "Go and buy it in, present it to his family, and send me the bill," said Mr. Heinz. They met on the street shortly afterward. Mr.—— held out his hand and said: "The man whom I treated as an enemy has proved to be my friend and saved me in my trouble."

Thus ended one of the most trying experiences of Mr. Heinz' life. He constantly declared his belief that mistakes or misfortunes often are blessings in disguise. He himself always tried to realize out of every bad experience something that should enable him to guard against the same happening again, and, as he put it, "turn defeat into victory." Many men were dragged down never to rise. He emerged from his misfortunes

A PERIOD OF TROUBLE

with greater ambition than before. Cautious and careful as he had been, he practiced thereafter a still greater caution, still greater carefulness—and, above all, he brought from the battle indomitable determination of will.

VII
BUILDING ANEW

He was thirty-one years old when disaster fell on him—a critical age when failure means to many men that they have suffered an irreparable calamity. He had a wife and two children, and he was penniless, for he had turned everything of his own over to his creditors. But he had a gift that remained with him, fresh and undimmed, to the hour of his death—a gift of youth. Through all his existence he looked toward Tomorrow with the interested spirit of a boy. So, though the disaster grieved him bitterly, his dismay was for others who had suffered through his firm's failure. For himself, he not only had the courage to face the necessity of beginning life all over again, but he lost no time in doing it. Less than two months after the failure of Heinz, Noble and Company, while still going through the heavy labor and deep tribulation of winding up its affairs, he started a new business in preparing food products.

BUILDING ANEW

It was going back to the beginning indeed; for it was again a tiny family venture, as the original vegetable garden had been. His brother John and his cousin Frederick Heinz each owned six shares of stock in a building and loan association, worth altogether $1600. With their faith in him strong as ever, they said: "We will give you our stock. You start in business, and we will work for you." He accepted, with the modification that instead of working for him, they were to have an interest in the business. His wife had left of her own means $400 in the bank and a mortgage on which his old friend and neighbor, Peter Prager, was willing to lend him $1000. With this total capital of $3000 the business was launched on February 6, 1876, under the name F. and J. Heinz, with himself as manager, since he could not conduct a business for himself till the courts had completed their slow process of granting him a discharge from bankruptcy.

It was arranged that Frederick and John should have one-sixth interest each. Because Mr. Heinz' parents had lost so heavily in endorsing the old firm's paper, the mother

BUILDING ANEW

was to have a one-sixth interest. His wife received a one-half interest, because of the money she had lost in helping the old firm meet its obligations, and in consideration of her share in advancing new capital.

When the owner of the building on Second Avenue which the old firm had occupied, and which had been closed on a landlord's warrant at the time of the failure, learned of the new business, he went to Mr. Heinz and suggested that he lease the house. To his objection that he did not know if he could afford to rent such a property, the owner replied: "You may take the building now without rent until April 1, and then lease by the year." So he rented the building on credit. There are men who always have credit. But he volunteered to spend for repairs an amount equal to the rent to April 1, because he believed in reciprocity.

Had the new firm offered stock for sale to investors, a very short paragraph would have been prospectus enough to name its tangible assets. Three thousand dollars capital did not provide a very impressive financial statement even in the days of smaller

BUILDING ANEW

things back in 1876. But it had greater resources. Many years later Mr. Heinz said: "It is neither capital nor labor that brings success, but management, because management can attract capital, and capital can employ labor."

The new firm was rich in management. It had a manager who was a creator, a builder, an economist, a trainer of men. He managed men without their knowing it. The note of self-reliance was dominant in him, always.

And if the new firm had little financial capital, it had another, and most precious, capital—good-will. There is only one way to get good-will. It is something that you get only by giving it. Henry Heinz had put his good-will into all that he had done for many years. Now it came back to him. It came back in the form of welcome from dealers who had done business with him. It came back in the form of willing purchases by the consumers who had learned to recognize that the name "Heinz" on a package of anything meant character.

Reduced to its concrete terms, quality is simply truth and genuineness. To a man

BUILDING ANEW

brought up to love the truth, these meanings became ingrained. He cannot think in other terms, and he imparts them to whatever he does. To Henry Heinz it would have been inconceivable to make anything less good than the best that he knew how to make. He said often: "Quality is to a product what character is to a man."

He abhorred the old legal maxim, heard with respect not so long ago in the law courts, "Caveat emptor" (Let the buyer beware). When he bought, he made sure of what he bought; but when he sold, he believed that it was his duty to take care of the buyer, to protect him against his own lack of knowledge, to give him the return that he ought to have for his investment. He went further. He realized always that to sell a man anything that he did not need, or more than he needed, was bad ethics and bad policy.

In the organization of the young business, Frederick Heinz was placed in charge of the gardening operations. He had been trained as florist and gardener in Germany, which at that time was famous for its thorough development of this science. He knew soils, seeds and fertilizers; he understood how to cultivate, how to co-operate with the laws of plant growth, and how to gather crops at their best. His fitness for the work was such that he remained in charge of it for thirty-six years, retiring in 1912, when old age at last obliged him to rest. He lived until 1922, revered and respected by all.

John Heinz took the position of superintendent of the manufacturing department. He was of a mechanical bent, and invented various devices of great practical usefulness. He stressed things rather than people, so he did not devote himself to managing the working staff. That work was done by the manager, who always was more interested in people than in anything else.

He held the curious idea—it was, indeed, accounted curious in those days—that good work is done only by happy, contented workers. Even if he had not had that queer idea, though, he would have striven to keep his people happy, anyway, for he was a worker himself, and he always thought of workers as working side by side with him,

BUILDING ANEW

rather than under him. So it was wholly spontaneous for him to be on friendly terms with all persons in the place. It was spontaneous for him to listen with interest to their recital of affairs at home, to sympathize with them when sorrow came to their families, to help when help was needed.

There is a placard on the walls of the Heinz offices today that expresses his belief and practice, from the very beginning of his career when he engaged his first employee to the days when the institution had more than six thousand:

FIND YOUR MAN, TRAIN YOUR
MAN, INSPIRE YOUR MAN, AND
YOU WILL KEEP YOUR MAN.

He believed in keeping men; and men did not willingly leave him. Long after his business had reached extremely large proportions, it was his pride that he knew every individual in the plant by name. He knew their family life, he knew how many children they had, he visited them when there was illness, and he was always ready for a plain,

BUILDING ANEW

man-to-man discussion of any points that they might raise about work or method.

If this had been done as a matter of mere astute and enlightened business policy, it might not have carried far. It certainly would not have built such an organization as he succeeded in building. As time went on, and he became a man prominent in commerce whose advice was sought eagerly by other business men, he thought much about industrial relations, and contributed many thoughts to American industry. But he never discovered, nor has anybody else ever discovered, a better way to make good industrial relations than the way he picked, half a century ago—the union of heart and head, with the heart never last.

It was this that made men want to stay with him even in the beginning when he had only hard work, and small reward, to offer. He held clever men who looked ahead with restless ambition, and he held simple people who looked for nothing further than the tasks for which they had been hired. From the top of today's organization down through all levels are people who began with him as

Henry J. Heinz    Howard Heinz

Sebastian Mueller    Clifford Heinz    W. H. Robinson    N. G. Woodside

J. N. Jeffares    Charles Heinz    H. C. Anderson    E. D. McCafferty

The Board of Directors of H. J. Heinz Company, 1919

BUILDING ANEW

youngsters. The board of directors is composed largely of men who started under him as boys. The first vice-president and general manager, the third vice-president, who is in charge of the company finances, the treasurer, the secretary and the assistant secretary, the superintendent of the Pittsburgh factory, and many others in high positions, all started with Mr. Heinz in his early days.

In the plant are many whose parents worked for him. One girl whom he employed in his small beginnings not only remained with him throughout, but one by one, as they became old enough, brought in her five sisters whom she was supporting. Mr. Heinz used to like to say that between them they raised her family; and it delighted him to tell how they all married from the institution, and how, in his latter years, he had the pleasure of seeing their children taking their places.

In charge of the many hundred girls employed in the main plant is a wonderful woman—wonderful for the indefatigable energy and enthusiasm that belie her seventy-odd years; wonderful for her influence over

BUILDING ANEW

the girls; wonderful, even in that institution, for the loyalty and love that she bears for the man who founded it. She is known to all, high and humble, by the affectionate title of just "Aggie." She was employed by Mr. Heinz in 1874. After some years of service, she married and went west. When her husband became ill, they returned to Pittsburgh, and he went to see them. Knowing that her husband could not live long, he said to her: "Remember that your old friends are your friends still, and be sure that we will save you from any hardships." She has been a member of what he used to call "the Heinz family" ever since. A short while before his death he met her on the street and said: "Aggie, you and I are growing old. I know you're strong. I'm strong, too. But I don't walk to business any more. We have to save ourselves a little." That day he gave orders that one of the company motor cars was to take her to and from the plant every day thereafter.

The up-building of the new business involved many other factors besides organization. As a business man, Mr. Heinz had

BUILDING ANEW

extraordinary talents, and he brought many original and great improvements into the work of distribution and selling. He knew what to make, how to make it, and how to sell it. He knew how to buy. He had genius for finance. But the story of the human organization is placed first here because it was the thought that was always first in his mind—first when he started in 1869, and first when he was the captain of an enormous institution.

The Main Plant at Pittsburgh Built Up by Henry J. Heinz

VIII

THE BUSINESS RECORD

THE history of the business after 1876 may be divided into three periods—the period 1876 to 1888, in which year the firm name became H. J. Heinz Company, the period following to 1905, when the partnership form was changed to the corporate form under the same name, and from 1905 to the present time.

During the years immediately following 1876 the establishment grew only as its manager felt satisfied to make a new step forward. With all his untiring energy, which made him an indefatigable worker, he still had a remarkable underlying patience. To outside observers his acts sometimes seemed paradoxical, because they did not understand that he utilized both these qualities of his. He moved quickly when it was time to move quickly. He moved slowly when it was best to do so. The men who grew up with him knew that when it came to doing anything swiftly and with every pound of driving force, he was easily the leader of the whole organization. But he saw no utility in bustle for the sake of bustle, or in doing something merely that there should be "something doing." He was absorbed in building, not in fireworks.

Therefore, he had unshakable patience for withholding action until the correct principle for the act had been established. This was his sole concern in the face of any problem. "The worst mistake you can make," he used to say to those under him, "is to let immediate convenience or comfort dictate a makeshift solution for any troublesome problem. Get at the fundamental principle involved, and settle your problem on that basis, and no other. The problem itself is nothing to worry about, no matter how big. In fact, the bigger the problem, the easier it is to see the principle on which it ought to be settled."

This same logic was behind that other apparent paradox in his character which led this man, who was ready at any moment to undertake huge undertakings without a tremor, to lay incessant, daily stress on the

THE BUSINESS RECORD

little things of life and business, and especially of production. Nothing was little to him when it involved a principle; but he had no patience with the petty mind that labors over petty details. One of his favorite illustrations was: "The trouble with most men is that they are looking all around for nickels that are scattered about them, when just ahead of them is a twenty-dollar gold piece."

He had that exceedingly rare talent which is talked of so glibly as if it were common—genius for detail. This so-called "genius for detail" means first of all the genius to know what details are important. There were many things that seem most important to the general type of business man, to which he paid no attention at all. Office routine was non-existent to him. His oldest associates can not remember that he ever spent twenty consecutive minutes at detail desk work. He could rarely be induced to listen to an elaborate financial statement. But he would spend hours in the plant with a group of workers over some seemingly trivial detail in the handling of food products. Anything

THE BUSINESS RECORD

connected with that work was vitally important to him, no matter how "little" it might seem to others.

He had true genius for finance; but Money never meant to him what Production meant. He was a producer first and foremost. The fruits of the earth meant something actually sacred to him. He had reverence for them. There was nothing connected with them, from the infinitesimal seed to the harvest, that was little to his mind; and so intense was this conviction that he succeeded in imbuing his entire organization with the same sense. The tiny organization of 1876 and the huge one that he lived to see—all were inspired by that dominant regard for the product of the earth as something precious.

So, though the years following 1876 saw a rapid growth, it still was a growth governed by patience. He had the patience to increase production only as he could train workers to produce as he wished it. He had the patience, and instilled some of it into his sales staffs, to wait for a man's business till it could be obtained on a principle that meant

THE BUSINESS RECORD

permanence. He had the patience to assure quality by building up the source of supply—the land and its methods of agriculture. It was not a wish to exploit, or ambition for increased possession, that led to continual expansion of land-holdings in every part of the continent, and in foreign lands. It occurred step after step as his standard for a certain crop demanded that it be raised and gathered under the conditions that he considered necessary.

When, in 1888, he took over the interest of his brother John, who wanted to go west, and became by title what he had been in fact for many years, the head of the firm, he was forty-four years old, and he might have accounted himself as a man who had arrived. His business was highly prosperous. He held an honored place in financial and commercial life. Under date of 1887 he had been able to record: "For years the paper of the house has been passing over the counters of the banks without an endorser or collateral." He had reached the point where he was able to contemplate the purchase of a stately home in the city that had known him as a poor boy. He might well have felt that he had reached his goal.

But prosperity did not mean a goal to him. He had no goal, in the sense that he ever set himself a mark at which he would be content to stop. Living was his goal, and his business meant to him an inseparable part of life and its duties. So his successes, financial and otherwise, made no difference. He went on, finding each new day a new and absorbing adventure; and in the thirty-one years between 1888 and his death in 1919, he reared an institution that made the success of 1888 seem almost tiny, and whose story is like the story of a complete life itself.

Incorporation was decided on in 1905 because the business had reached a magnitude that made the change desirable and advantageous. From time to time new partners had been admitted, and other partners had retired or died. Among the latter was his mother, who had long been called "Mother Heinz" by all. It was felt that in place of the termination of a partnership, and the necessary reorganization, there was needed

THE BUSINESS RECORD

the perpetuity of existence which the corporation form provides.

Under this change, the existing partners became the stockholders of the new company: Henry J. Heinz; his cousin, Frederick Heinz; his son, Howard Heinz; his brother-in-law, Sebastian Mueller, and two old associates, W. H. Robinson and R. G. Evans. Mr. Heinz became the first president and held that office till death.

The change in form wrought no change in spirit, purpose or ideals. It still was a "family" enterprise. It remained an institution of direct personal relations from top to bottom. When its form assumed that of a corporation, it was of that kind which never ceased to excite the admiration of England's great jurist, Lord Coke, when he referred to it as "an intellect without decline, a body without death, a soul with a purpose that ever inspires."

When on December 20, 1919, a few months after his death, the company commemorated his career and fifty years of business progress with a banquet given by the board of directors to the employees, and

THE BUSINESS RECORD

when the speakers' list contained such names as Judge Joseph Buffington of the U. S. Circuit Court of Appeals, William C. Sproul, Governor of Pennsylvania; Harry Wheeler, President of the United States Chamber of Commerce, and Charles M. Schwab, chairman of the board of the Bethlehem Steel Corporation, there were given the following statistics of the organization that Mr. Heinz had reared:

Employees	6,523
Harvesters of crops we use	100,000
Branch Factories, including one each in Canada, England and Spain	25
Pickle Salting Stations	85
Raw Product Receiving Stations	87
Railroad Cars Owned and Operated	258
Carloads of Goods Handled, 1919	17,011
Acres to Grow our Crops	100,000
Salesmen	952
Branch Offices and Warehouses	55

THE BUSINESS RECORD

Agencies in all the Leading Commercial Centers of the World.

We own and operate our own Bottle Factory, Box Factories and Tin Can Factory, as well as our own Seed Farms.

And the policy of this great enterprise today? It is as Mr. Heinz stated it when a group of financiers proposed to buy it, offering the argument that he had worked all his life and should "cash in"—get a good big price and enjoy the leisure to which he was entitled. It was an alluring proposal as they outlined it. He heard it all out, and answered promptly:

"I do not care for your money, neither do I nor my family wish to go out of business. We are not looking for ease or rest or freedom from responsibility. I love this business. Your talk of more money and less responsibility means nothing to me. To stop work is death—mentally and physically. This business is run, not for my family or a few families, but for what we call the Heinz family—the people who make our goods

THE BUSINESS RECORD

and sell them. The Heinz policy is to work for a better business rather than a bigger business; to make, if possible, a better product, and to make better people as we go along. We are working for success, and not for money. The money part will take care of itself."

IX
ELEMENTS OF HIS PERSONALITY

In what has been written, many of the characteristics of Mr. Heinz appear. Some he had in common with other men, but his personality had, in words applied to another, "its own distinctive tang." Although his figure was not tall in stature, he had personality plus. No one ever asked, "Is he anybody in particular?" He was somebody in particular—all over and all the time.

No person who ever met him in even the most casual way could fail to perceive his genial disposition. He loved a smile. Once he taught the value of a smile in an unusual way. A young man, bright and with character, occupied a position that brought him into contact with a great many people who called at the office. But he could not smile. Mr. Heinz looked around the establishment, found a young man who could smile, and made him assistant to number one. He said to the head of the department that number two did not have the ability to

ELEMENTS OF HIS PERSONALITY

do the work, but his smile would attract, and number one would do the work. At the end of the month the salary of number two was advanced, and number one wondered why he had not received this mark of favor. When an opportunity came to explain to the disappointed young man, Mr. Heinz said, "I can afford to pay for his smile. It is worth something to me to have someone in the office who can meet strangers with a smile." The news spread through the place that Mr. Heinz was advancing salaries for those who could smile. Smiling became popular. "It's good business," said he, "to employ men who smile."

By nature and training he was democratic. He admired simple things and simple ways. He had love for what are known as the "plain people." To them he was always attracted and attached. He realized that with them there was the greater opportunity to help them to do the things that would broaden their outlook, widen their vision, and lift them up to the appreciation of higher ideals and finer aspirations. He was never happier in Christian work than when

ELEMENTS OF HIS PERSONALITY

associated with a congregation poor in resources and few in numbers. The great congregation, with influential membership and large means, did not afford an equal opportunity for helpfulness—and to help someone who needed help was a purpose he kept constantly in view.

He would listen to suggestions from the humblest source. An office boy was made as free to approach him as his partners. He always had time to listen, and he never dismissed a suggestion, even though it was valueless on its face, without discussing it with the one who made it. He had the hospitable mind; was ready to receive an idea from anyone, peer, employee or stranger. He had the power to adapt ideas to his business, as few men have.

For what is usually known as "Society" he had little inclination. But he loved social intercourse and he made his home the place of many informal dinners, where charming friendship held sway. There was nothing exclusive about him. His accessibility was a characteristic. He denied himself to no one

ELEMENTS OF HIS PERSONALITY

having a just claim on his time. To the president of a large corporation, or to the humble rural Sunday School teacher, he was equally cordial and considerate. The onlooker could not detect any difference in his reception of the mighty and the humble. He had a great respect for a human being simply because he was a human being.

He went to great lengths to keep a man who had promise, or whose character could be improved; but he evinced no weakness toward those whose characters were proved to be bad. Thus, one of his branch managers, after serious misconduct due largely to drink, was warned that repetition would entail immediate discharge. He repeated the offense. Mr. Heinz instructed the sales manager to dismiss him at once. "His wife and child are in the hospital, and he is penniless," pleaded the sales manager. "Dismiss him at once!" repeated Mr. Heinz. Then, when he saw that his order was understood and accepted as imperative, he said: "That's business. The other matter is charity. Draw the necessary money, and look after the wife and child."

ELEMENTS OF HIS PERSONALITY

Though he held a recognized position as one of the active fighters against the evil of drink, and though he insisted on sobriety in those whom he employed, he made it clear to them that he demanded it as a matter of good business conduct, and not because he took it on himself to dictate the personal habits of other men. Men who knew of his deep religious zeal often expected when they first entered into business relations with him, that he would preach to them, and otherwise, perhaps, endeavor to regulate their spiritual attitude. But the same simple regard for other men's rights and feelings that governed him in other relations governed him in this, his deepest conviction. He respected other men's creeds, other men's beliefs, and even their disbeliefs; and he was especially thoughtful of this in the case of those on whom he might most easily have exerted some pressure.

He had utter courage, physical and moral. He had the courage as a business man to make his religion and religious ethics a part of business. He had the courage as a churchman to make tolerance a part of his religion.

ELEMENTS OF HIS PERSONALITY

The fear of criticism never moved him. No fears ever did. He was afraid of being wrong, but of nothing else. Once he was convinced that a given course was right, he could not be turned from it.

When he was convinced, his conviction became an enthusiasm that burned with a vital flame. It was, indeed, like a white heat that fused all his organization to one purpose. So intense was it that few men could stand up against it. Opposition was half defeated before it asserted itself. Yet, though he had such personal force, he tried always to win other men to his way rather than to dominate them. "Don't you think we'd better do so-and-so?" was his habitual way of appeal.

There was one exception. He would neither debate nor compromise in any matter of moral principle. On such a point he was a Caesar. His fist smashed down on desk or table, and no man dared to contradict or even to argue.

He was a fighting man by nature. He loved a contest, a hard tussle, a battle. But he had trained himself to be a peacemaker.

ELEMENTS OF HIS PERSONALITY

Everywhere—in committees, on boards of directors, in social service activities, in public meetings where ideas and interests were bitterly opposed—men said that when Henry Heinz arose there would be a stilling of discord. He could, and did, become stirred to great angers; and no man with one experience of these willingly incurred another. But he had so inculcated in himself the habit of peace that again and again he maintained it in the face of bitter aggravation.

Of this acquired treasure of inner peace he made a power. He made it a power not only for himself, but for winning men and holding them to him, for helping and strengthening them. In his organization today one can hear many stories of how he, so well capable of giving battle, conquered other men not by outfighting them, not by answering blow with blow, but with his peace.

Among his employees was one, his coachman, who was noted throughout Pittsburgh for his amazing and utter fidelity. His devotion to Mr. Heinz was so deep and complete that it is no figure of speech to say that

ELEMENTS OF HIS PERSONALITY

he would at any time have given his life for the man whom he was proud to call his master. Yet in an earlier period this man had been feared because of a temper whose fury knew no bounds. The story of how he was conquered illustrates the method that made Mr. Heinz successful with his employees.

One day, in one of his sudden furies, this coachman struck a horse with a shovel. Mr. Heinz happened to be at home that day, and all who knew his love of horses expected a storm. He controlled himself, and busied himself with some other things about the place, until he was quite sure that the coachman would know of his presence, and be concerned as to what was going to happen to him. The man was nearly sick with anticipation, and at last in the afternoon his employer walked into the stable and said, with a smile: "Albert, I have been wanting to tell you how I liked your team on Sunday; your horses never looked better. They were shining."

The man was dumb with amazement and hung his head, for that was not what he had been expecting. Mr. Heinz continued: "I

ELEMENTS OF HIS PERSONALITY

was proud of that team. Everything was right about it. The harness was perfect. Albert, I have always felt that you were one of the best coachmen in the city."

The coachman drew a breath of relief and began to raise his head. Then Mr. Heinz stepped close to him, put his hand on his shoulder and said: "Now, Albert, I want to talk with you about a personal matter—about a little thing that I know must cause you a great deal of concern. Temper is absolutely essential in any real man. I like temper; but, if it is not controlled, it is a destructive force. Now I want to plan with you how we are going to work out a method of controlling your temper."

The tears that came to the man's eyes were better to Mr. Heinz than words.

"Oh, how can you forgive me?" he asked. "I was sure I was going to be discharged. I never realized before how serious a handicap a bad temper was, and I promise that I will control it hereafter."

Although all with whom he dealt knew that they might appeal to his forbearance, his talent for handling men was such that

ELEMENTS OF HIS PERSONALITY

they understood clearly that it meant no laxness of discipline. He, himself, had so made discipline a part of his own life that it was inevitable that he should make it, as he did, a supreme factor in building up and governing his organization. He insisted on discipline; but he maintained it as he built up other factors of the institution—by making men understand it. They knew that he did not want them to fear him, but that he was a man to be most thoroughly feared if occasion was given to him.

Thus, there were details of business discipline whose infraction he would never treat with equanimity or forbearance. Anything connected with the handling of the product, from raw material to the package, had to be done just so. Anything affecting the credit of the institution was equally a matter of inviolable discipline. Delay in paying any obligation, even though it were only a short or accidental delay, was intolerable to him. His organization still remembers an occasion, though it was many years ago. He happened to be in one of the factory buildings at the moment when the pay-roll money was due.

ELEMENTS OF HIS PERSONALITY

He waited, watch in hand, for exactly five minutes. Then he dashed across the courtyard to the offices, and—well, as said, they remember it still.

As a small boy he had learned to be punctilious in meeting obligations and keeping promises. He often told the following story:

"On one occasion my father borrowed a small sum from an acquaintance, because there was no bank in the village. He promised to repay it on a Saturday. On Friday he told my mother that he must hurry out to settle the debt. 'Why,' said my mother, 'you said it was due tomorrow.' 'Margaret,' said my father, 'you know that when I say that I will pay on a given day, I always pay the day before.'"

Once Mr. Heinz saw a man turning from the cashier's window and folding up an invoice. He hurried over and asked the cashier if he had paid the bill. "No," was the reply. "We didn't have the money, and he was in no hurry." "That has nothing to do with the matter," said Mr. Heinz. "It's our business to pay every bill that is due the moment it's presented. Go out the next time, if necessary, to borrow the money from a bank; but get it, and pay what we owe."

Prompt pay was an impulse of his character. He was ready at any time to fulfill an obligation, and in fact did so many times when it meant loss that might have been avoided by a small delay. But prompt pay was also recognized by him as one of the best business builders. He never made the blunder of believing that any gain of value came from holding on to money to the last possible moment. His definition of prompt pay was "Living Credit." He knew, and proved, that a reputation for prompt payment gained important advantages in price, delivery and discounts.

In the currency panic of 1908 his first step was to borrow very large sums, though he did not actually need the funds to meet any obligations. He used them to build up the company's bank balances all over the country, so that there could be no difficulty in getting cash in any amount, if needed. The interest that he had to pay on these "unnecessary" loans was nothing to him when compared with the value of maintaining

ELEMENTS OF HIS PERSONALITY

spotless credit. He said it was the cheapest kind of good insurance.

There is here another illustration of the extraordinary duality of nature that enabled him to attend to, and take concentrated pleasure in, all the countless little things of production, day after day, and yet never let any amount of detail obscure the big thing. To him the big thing always seemed the easiest thing to do. "Anybody can see the big things," he used to say. "But some day somebody will get a big salary in this institution for doing nothing except to look after the little things."

Most men who were to take on themselves the mounting responsibility for the innumerable details of work in such a business as that of handling delicate and perishable food products would find it a heavy load to carry. He did it through more than half a century, with never-failing zest and vigor, and yet never did he miss seeing "the instant need of things" when a big and daring action was to be undertaken. But because during that half century he had built an organization imbued with his own conscientious regard for little things, he could conceive the big thing in a big way, with the confidence that he could trust its execution in detail to the men he had trained.

So there was the paradox that the same man who would, and did, spend an hour in lecturing his organization about waste would, in the next five minutes, direct the spending of thousands of dollars for some good object. "All the money necessary for a useful purpose, but not a cent for waste," might have been one of his mottoes.

He had vitality for work that seemed inexhaustible. His apparently slight physique deceived men who did not know that he had a very considerable amount of muscular strength as well as a sound constitution. His activity was such that those who were closely associated with him cannot remember him except as moving about, quickly, incessantly alive, rarely sitting down, and then only till some new thought or errand started him off again in a march through the office departments or a long journey through the huge plant. As may be inferred, he was a tireless walker. He made no cult of health, but he

ELEMENTS OF HIS PERSONALITY

valued it. His simplicity and frugality of diet were a part of his natural simplicity of life, and not due primarily to considerations of hygiene. But he knew how to live sanely, and he tried to do it.

He did not, however, try to conserve energy. He seemed to thrive on expending it, and he never drained it, for he displayed as much vital force in the last year of his life as if he were a young man. It was this abounding, apparently inexhaustible, vital energy that enabled him on his busiest day, in the midst of pressing engagements, to give his whole attention, and his whole hearty personal interest, to an acquaintance whom he might meet by chance.

This busy man—one of the genuinely busy men of America—who could not find time enough in any day or in all lifetime for all that he wanted to do—always had time to stop to cheer somebody on his way. Especially was this the case with children. His love for them was so complete and wide that it gathered all children—his own and every waif on the street—in one great embrace of affection. To say that he never passed a child

ELEMENTS OF HIS PERSONALITY

on the street without speaking to it seems like saying too much; yet many in his institution declare that they cannot remember that he did. At any rate, it had to be a desperately important errand that would prevent him from stopping at least a moment to pat a child on the head and give it a little token.

In his pockets, in his desk at the office, in his desk at home, he maintained a little stock of gifts—pictures, books, illuminated cards—for them. "He loved children more than any man I ever knew," says one of his fellow directors. "I never saw him happier than when he was doing some such thing as helping a lot of kids shoot off fireworks on the Fourth of July or celebrating some other holiday. And they loved him. He could win the confidence of any one of them. The way children used to come to the plant—you know the Heinz establishment is always open to visitors—you'd think that all the youngsters in Pittsburgh had passed the word around. And I don't think that he ever saw a child without giving it something."

"If he met children in the streets near the

ELEMENTS OF HIS PERSONALITY

plant," says another, "his first question would be: 'Do your people work here?' Often he would come into a directors' meeting, his face radiant, to repeat what some child had said: how a father or mother, or both, or other relatives, had told at home of the way the plant was conducted, and of their pleasure in the work."

A man who could fight, but who preferred to shake hands; an intensely practical, shrewd man who was not afraid of sentiment; a man who demanded punctilious fulfillment of duty from everybody, and yet who forgave inferior service if the spirit was right; that was Henry Heinz. None insisted more on discipline, and none ever was more quickly and implicitly obeyed. But he won service by being loved, not by being feared.

All his instincts ran to cheerful informality of intercourse. Yet he was a man with whom no person would dream of taking a liberty. He did not carry a sense of dignity around with him. His character was his dignity. He was so unconscious of it, and yet so secure in its possession, that he did not have to panoply himself with the armor of

ELEMENTS OF HIS PERSONALITY

place and rank. He could afford to be simply, endearingly, intelligently human, and he was. He could afford to offer every man good humor and kindliness, and he did.

Human kindness was not a mere trait. It was himself. It was his constant thought to give pleasure to others. He lived the truth which often found expression from his lips: "We get out of life what we put into it." He put into it love and service and kindness, and he took out of it, in unstinted measure, compensation in kind.

X

AN ENDURING STRUCTURE

BY achieving an eminent business success, he demonstrated that thorough ethics and thoroughly sound, practical business methods are wholly compatible. A still greater fact which he demonstrated was that such ethics, which seem at first sight intensely individual and personal, can be infused throughout a whole great organization, and can become so deeply implanted that they are self-perpetuating.

A cardinal article of his faith was that men can be trusted, that most men would rather do right than wrong. He perceived that the reason they did not adhere to their best inclinations was that they were afraid they could not succeed that way in business.

His big deed of human leadership was to show men that they did not need to be afraid. He showed them that the belief that business demanded ruthlessness and the cutting of moral corners was a superstition as foolish as it was evil. He built a business that proved it. From the time when he gathered around

AN ENDURING STRUCTURE

him his first associates he inspired them with the same faith, and so imbued them with it that they in turn inspired the new men directly under them.

The institution that he founded stands as a triumphant justification of this tenet that principles and ethics are the imperishable factors of business organization and permanence. In the fifty-four years of its existence there necessarily have been many changes in individual membership; but always, now as in the beginning, the organization has gone on unchanged, with successors ready to conduct it on the same lines.

Mr. Heinz never picked men simply to work under him. He picked them to work with and after him. He studied youngsters to find among them chiefs of the future. Long before they themselves dreamed of such promotion he had picked men to be his partners and was training them with infinite care and patience. Reference already has been made to the fact that most of the present officers of the company and members of the board of directors are men who began with him in their youth, and that throughout the

Experience and Getting Experience—Henry J. Heinz and His Three Sons

AN ENDURING STRUCTURE

organization in all parts of the country men whom he trained as lads are holding important positions.

He did not content himself with training them simply as direct successors. He trained them to train their successors, to build on and on, in his faith that "heart-power is better than horse-power," and that an institution which strives primarily to win the hearts of its employees can safely count on the best work of their heads and hands.

Thus, he succeeded in transmitting his spirit, as living today as if his mortal body were present. It is vivid in the minds of many men who believe as he did, who would not conduct business in any other way, and who echo every word of his business policy.

Much of what is being done in the Heinz institution is today accepted by the world as a part of wisdom in industrial relations. But it was not so when Mr. Heinz began it. He was a pioneer in what is now called "welfare work" among employees. He did not call it that. He did not call it by any name. He did not do it to head off unrest. In his mind it was not connected with wage questions or other labor problems. He did it because he thought it was right; because he thought of himself as a fellow worker, and knew the priceless value of willing spirit—and by willing spirit he meant that the employer's spirit must be as willing as that of the employee.

So he was among the first employers in the country to provide such comforts as diningrooms, locker-rooms and dressing-rooms. His intense insistence on meticulous neatness and cleanliness in everything pertaining to food products led him to originate many innovations in industry. Instead of trying to enforce it merely by rigorous orders and discipline, he offered facilities and conveniences as his share of the duty, and thus made it a matter of mutual benefit. He inaugurated the idea of providing clean, fresh working uniforms for the women, a system which had the advantage for them of saving their street garments, in addition to giving them more comfort while at work. He installed a manicurist department, which so appealed to the natural womanly desire for well-tended hands that they took pride in the inspections and other exacting rules that

AN ENDURING STRUCTURE

are laid down for all who handled material in the plant.

A "first-aid" station for service in case of accidents as well as rest and recreation rooms were early features. He soon went further. He told the employees that if it paid to give them aid in the plant when they were injured, he thought it would pay the institution to give them aid in general matters of health, and he offered them a trained nurse and a doctor. To this medical establishment there was soon added a dentist, who does dentistry work free for all employees. Mr. Heinz was an early discoverer of the loss of time and suffering due to defective teeth.

In every way he tried to make the surroundings bear out his idea that the working day should be happy. Paintings and other objects were installed to satisfy the love for beauty. The cheerfulness and freshness of growing things were brought to the plant through window boxes of flowers and in other forms. He tried to make the place a place to live in as well as work in.

Years before such undertakings were considered as anything but visionary, he built

AN ENDURING STRUCTURE

an auditorium in the plant, for lectures, motion pictures, dramatic performances, singing and music, as well as for dancing and other amusements initiated by the employees themselves.

It was his regular custom to come before the employees in the auditorium and discuss working conditions, changes of method, such as hours of employment, the general conditions of business throughout the country, and other topics bearing on the mutual interest. During the war his inspiring talks in the campaigns for raising various war funds led them to go "over the top" in such form that they were always one hundred per cent in their Red Cross and other contributions.

He was one of the first employers to introduce free life insurance. Both the recreational and the educational ideas were among those that took practical form years ago. A swimming pool, a gymnasium and a roof garden are in the plant group. Sewing and cooking classes for the women and mechanical drawing lessons for the men are among the group activities.

AN ENDURING STRUCTURE

He was extremely fond of anything that fostered the intra-social spirit, and he made a great annual occasion of the yearly picnic, which he often planned for some quite distant point, so that the employees and their families might enjoy new surroundings and scenery. The "57 Clubs," one the Men's 57 Club, and the other the Girls' 57 Club, are social clubs in which he was keenly interested, and they have been developed to a point where they play a great part in the spirit of "the Heinz family." A monthly newspaper for the employees and a dramatic society are part of their activities.

In these, and the many other provisions for the comfort and happiness of those in the plant, he was most careful always to so initiate them and administer them that there was no suggestion of their being handed down from on high as acts of grace or charity. He made them all matters of genuine fellowship, springing normally and naturally from the union of employer and employees. He showed such unflagging and unreserved personal delight in them, day by day, that

AN ENDURING STRUCTURE

they became, and remain, like bonds that tie an actual family together.

To his spirit of personal participation, the Christmas season was particularly significant, and the custom of joint Christmas celebration by employer and employees is an old one in the Heinz plant, dating back more than forty years. Even in the early days of struggle he could not have gone home with a happy heart on Christmas Eve had he not given each employee something, if not more than a jar of preserves. As prosperity grew, the gifts grew; but big or little, whether simply a token as in the old days, or handsome presents such as silk umbrellas, silk scarfs, specially made Swiss clocks and so on, they were given in the spirit of the family celebration. Little Christmas trees in each department, personal greetings and interchange of good wishes between officers of the company and employees, mutual participation of all throughout the organization in personal interchange of gifts—these make the annual festival a real one.

The sense of unity typified by these interrelations was expressed by the employees in

AN ENDURING STRUCTURE

1909 when the celebration of the fortieth anniversary of the business was seized by them as the occasion for giving him a most beautiful silver loving cup, with words of affection that he treasured deeply:

TO
HENRY J. HEINZ

FORTIETH ANNIVERSARY
of
H. J. HEINZ COMPANY

A TOKEN OF AFFECTIONATE REGARD AND ESTEEM
from your
DIRECTORS AND EMPLOYEES

XI

BUSINESS POLICIES

He was not a dreamer or a visionary, who went into business and by chance made a success. He was a business man by origin, by preference, by training. He brought into business his own unique philosophy of business, but he used the same machinery of business that always has been used. He bought carefully. He produced with efficiency. He sold effectively. He expected those with whom he dealt to fulfill agreements as he fulfilled his. His success was on regular business lines, not by any revolutionary method such as only a genius may, now and then, apply for a short-lived term.

He brought about decided changes in the business methods of handling and selling prepared food products, but all these changes were based on the same steady principles of practical and sound business that all men recognize.

A notable example is his successful fight against the practice of "sale of futures" which was dominant in the industry. It had been a custom of pickling establishments to sell for future delivery, the sellers speculating on a large coming crop with low prices for their raw material, and the buyers speculating on the opposite.

To Mr. Heinz any business transaction in which all parties did not benefit equitably was not only wrong as practical business, but morally wrong. In buying and selling futures, both parties could not possibly profit. Somebody had to lose every season.

He told his organization that he intended to fight. "No man can fix an honest price on his product," he said, "till he knows what it is going to cost him, and no man can know that till he knows what the crop is."

His sales force, willing as a rule to follow him in anything, was taken aback. The men protested that if the Heinz organization, all alone, waited till the crop was ready to pick before taking orders, all the dealers would be loaded up by the time the Heinz salesmen entered the market. He recognized that they were arguing with loyal regard for his interests, and he pursued his usual course. He resolved to convince them by experience.

BUSINESS POLICIES

All the information that he had gathered led him to anticipate that the next crop would be unusually short, with correspondingly high prices for raw material. He permitted his men to meet the market practice of selling futures, and waited. The crop turned out to be so small that prices soared. When the season's business was finished, he called in the sales managers from all parts of the country and showed them the books. Their sales for future delivery, on a price made in advance of the crop, had cost the company $100,000.

From that day, the whole organization stood with him like a rock against future sales, and in the end succeeded in educating the dealers to buy when the price could be set fairly and intelligently.

He paid a large sum to gain his end; but he had calculated it in advance, and had decided, correctly, that it would come back in the form of better business. And with the speculative element eliminated, the road was clear for the next sweeping reform, which was to keep the dealers' stocks down to those quantities that they should have for quick turnovers. It was a new conception to salesmen—to advise customers to buy less rather than more, and many dealers were almost as hard to convince. He inaugurated the new policy with another object lesson, by instructing his salesmen to inform dealers that the company would return to them fifty per cent of the purchase price for goods that had been in their stocks for a period that he considered too long for retaining full perfection of flavor. As fast as the salesmen could take them over, they broke them up on the spot for the rubbish heap.

It cost another large sum of money. But the stores of the entire country were cleared of old stock. The consumer everywhere was sure to get the Heinz quality he had learned to expect. The dealers were freed from the burden and waste of carrying over-stocks, which mean dead stocks and ultimate loss.

The policy bore rich fruit for both dealers and the company in the reconstruction period after 1918. When the vast climb of prices began during the war the business world apparently had only one thought—to buy, buy, buy, stock up to the limit. In that wild

BUSINESS POLICIES

time this policy did not seem wild. It seemed the best business. The catastrophe of Europe had so affected human psychology that all the accustomed judgments and reasonings of mankind were shaken.

Henry J. Heinz looked at that orgy which was called a "seller's market." He saw that men were so determined to buy that all lines were broken. If he would not sell to them, they would buy from others. It was not a question of quality, or old relations, or anything else just then except delivery—delivery of anything and everything.

He recognized all this—and the Heinz institution sent word to all its salesmen to cut sales to current requirements only.

To the dealers the information came as exceedingly unwelcome news. But when the downward turn of prices began they had low inventories of Heinz goods. And the Heinz institution, though it had sacrificed huge possible sales for the time, also had low inventories, and was able to put out the new lower prices immediately. The result was that during the long period of deflation, when innumerable concerns reported no orders at all and millions of dollars had to be written off as losses due to depreciation in inventories, the Heinz organization had a small minor depreciation to write off, and its business showed a very considerable increase. The customers realized with profound satisfaction that they had no stocks of Heinz goods on which to take losses.

These, and the many other policies that he put through during his long career, were all with a view beyond the immediate present. They looked to the future—future business, future stability, future good-will. And they succeeded and had permanent results because they were for the mutual advantage of all concerned. When he sold, he thought of the profit for the dealer and the satisfaction of the consumer. When he bought, he considered the interests of the seller as well as his own. The buying staffs of the Heinz organization today repeat his cardinal rule: "Deal with the seller so justly that he will want to sell to you again." He bought shrewdly, and few men knew so well as he the exact state of a market; but one of the traditions of the buying department is that

BUSINESS POLICIES

the men of whom he bought most closely were his staunchest friends and admirers.

His selling policies were on the same principle. Long before the merchants of the United States heard such phrases as "merchandising service," he was acting on the idea that it is not enough for a manufacturer to get his goods on a merchant's shelves, but that he must help get them off the shelves again. Therefore, he sought the good-will of the consumer by every means possible.

Advertising was one of the instrumentalities that he utilized to an ever-growing extent. The story of the development of this one activity alone would be almost a history of the evolution of American advertising, for it would record a beginning with a few inexpensive, simple cards and signs, and lead up to the present organized publicity, utilizing almost every sound advertising element and keeping the company's name and products before all countries and races of the world where commerce penetrates.

He had no training or experience in advertising when he began. But he had the faculty of speaking to people in their own language;

he knew exactly what he wanted to tell them, and he did not want to tell them anything except what he believed himself. So from the first, his advertising had the greatest quality that advertising can have—sincerity. It is the vital spark of advertising, and it can not be faked. The insincere man may use words that glitter, but somehow, in a way not to be defined, the sincere man will get something foursquare into his plain statements, and the other fellow cannot.

As with other parts of his business, he moved slowly and cautiously till he had learned, and then he advanced swiftly. In the course of a few decades the little advertising department that had turned out a few street-car cards had grown to a department that conducted some of the largest outdoor display advertising in the country.

When he turned to the field of printed advertising, he again wanted to learn slowly, though by that time he had become one of the largest outdoor advertisers of the country. When his son proposed the first magazine campaign, he said: "How much do you want?" The answer was: "Twenty-five

Heinz Ocean Pier, Atlantic City

BUSINESS POLICIES

thousand dollars." "We begin slowly here," said Mr. Heinz. "I will let you have ten thousand dollars." When he saw the result he said: "Good! How much do you want now?" The answer was: "A hundred thousand dollars." "I will give you twenty-five thousand," said he. After that, when the test had satisfied him, he was ready to go into that form of advertising in the same big way as the other.

At the World's Fair Exposition in Chicago he saved not only his own display, but the exhibits of all the food-product makers represented there, from what looked like hopeless failure. They had been placed in a gallery, and as soon as the Exposition opened it became sadly evident that of the army of visitors only melancholy driblets would climb there. Everybody, including the managers of the Exposition, bowed to what seemed beyond remedy. Mr. Heinz spent an evening pondering. Next week visitors walking through the grounds were startled by spying brass trunk checks here and there. They picked them up and saw the apparent checks bore an announcement that the finder

BUSINESS POLICIES

would receive a souvenir at the Heinz booth.

There were thousands of checks. The rush to the food-products exhibit became so great that in the end it was necessary to strengthen the supports of the gallery. Once the tide had turned, it kept flowing. The exhibit was amply interesting, even without souvenirs, and through the whole period of the Exposition the food-product gallery remained one of the popular attractions. One of Mr. Heinz' prized possessions was a loving cup that the other food-product men gave him in recognition of the success that he had snatched out of failure for them all.

The famous Atlantic City Pier advertisement is another of his conceptions. It is undoubtedly correct to say that there is no other single advertisement like it in the world, for the Heinz advertisement in that great pleasure city is an entire pier, beflagged in the day time, burning bright and white with electricity at night, with rest-rooms and lecture-hall, a collection of art and antiques, display rooms and demonstration space. Every day throughout the year it is crowded

BUSINESS POLICIES

with visitors, and as Atlantic City has an immense daily influx of people from all parts of the American Continent, not to count foreign visitors, this one advertisement may well be considered a very substantial national campaign by itself.

In all the company's advertising, the phrase "57 Varieties" is so familiar to all America that it has become the universally recognized symbol of the Heinz products. Its origin was in 1896. Mr. Heinz, while in an elevated railroad train in New York, saw among the car-advertising cards one about shoes with the expression "21 Styles." It set him to thinking, and as he told it: "I said to myself, 'we do not have styles of products, but we do have varieties of products.' Counting up how many we had, I counted well beyond 57, but '57' kept coming back into my mind. 'Seven, seven'—there are so many illustrations of the psychological influence of that figure and of its alluring significance to people of all ages and races that '58 Varieties' or '59 Varieties' did not appeal at all to me as being equally strong. I got off the train immediately, went down to the

BUSINESS POLICIES

lithographer's, where I designed a street-car card and had it distributed throughout the United States. I myself did not realize how highly successful a slogan it was going to be."

All these widely branching business activities—buying, manufacturing, selling, distributing, shipping and advertising—were bound together into close unity. He was a pioneer in the holding of conventions of his salesmen and other departments. Personal contact was all-important to him. He believed it to be a thousandfold more effective than correspondence. In 1902 he brought his salesmen from all over the world together in Pittsburgh, the convention numbering almost four hundred men. Since the early years of the '80's there has been at each Branch House a monthly convention of all Branch House Salesmen, country and city. There has been a semi-annual convention of Branch House Managers and Head Salesmen ever since that period. Branch House Head Salesmen meet in weekly convention. Every quarter year there has been a convention of Branch House District Managers. In addition to these there are conventions of

BUSINESS POLICIES

District Salting House Managers, Branch Factory Managers, Heads of Departments, and many others. In fact, the policy of constant personal contact and mutual exchange of information and ideas was brought by him into every part and corner of the business, and its maintenance today is one of the most powerful factors for the smooth working of the big institution.

XII

HOME AND THE FAMILY FIRESIDE

His love for children was more than fond sentiment. He understood them. The study of their minds was an absorbing pursuit. Everything that interested them had his own eager interest. He seemed to know intuitively how a child sees things, and because of this children understood him. They had confidence in him. "No matter what our father asked us to do or not to do," says one of his sons, "we never felt that it was hard or unfair." As they recall their infancy, they recall him even then not at all as a conventional father, but as a trusted companion—one to whom it was natural to tell everything.

The secret of his success as a father is that he took joy in human life. As some men love and study books, he loved and studied human beings. He delighted in the duty of fellowship, and in his home he imparted something of that joy to his children. He never held duty up before them as a stern commandment. He showed it to them as happiness, and every day he himself was

HOME AND THE FAMILY FIRESIDE

their best example, because they could not fail to see the pleasure that he got from every duty well performed, every responsibility well borne.

In the Heinz house the words "must" and "must not" were so rare that it might almost be said they did not exist. He wanted to get results at home, as he did in business, not by compelling obedience, but by winning it. He sought to develop his children by developing in them willingness of heart.

He taught them unity of existence. His business life and his family life were not separate phases with a gulf between. He had no business face or business manner that he needed to shed when he entered the door of his home. He did not bring his business home in the sense of dragging a chain, but the fortunes of the working day, and the lives and fortunes of the people in the institution, were part of the family interest. His children never heard anything to suggest that the duties, problems and satisfactions of life at home were different from the duties and satisfactions of the working part of life.

HOME AND THE FAMILY FIRESIDE

In maintaining this unity of life, he had a partner in the deepest and sweetest sense of the word. Sarah Sloan Young, who became his wife on September 23, 1869, loved and understood children as he did, and she loved and understood him. To a beautifully serene disposition she united a wit that was unmistakably a happy racial inheritance from her parents' lineage which ran back through many generations in County Down, Ireland.

In the early days of their married life, when he was fighting hard to establish himself, he had formed the habit of doing some work at home practically every evening. After he had reached success, he continued it, usually by bringing home somebody with whom he wished to discuss matters. She did not try, as some fond wives might do, to dissuade him. She knew that his zeal was a part of him. She had ready for him amusing stories of her day's experiences. She saw to it that there should be a romp with the children, and that the talk at dinner should be such as to give him utter relaxation.

Throughout their married life these two thus smoothed every road for each other.

HOME AND THE FAMILY FIRESIDE

The recollection of her unfailing courage and support in the days of adversity was his richest treasure of memory. Their first modest home in Sharpsburg was as dear to their thoughts as the noble house that they came to inhabit later. They were bound together, one and complete, from beginning to end.

In that first home in Sharpsburg two children were born to them. The first was Irene Edwilda, who became the wife of John L. Given of New York.

The second child, Clarence, was born April 17, 1873. After his school days he served in the business till failure of health compelled his retirement. He died, unmarried, in 1920.

The third child, Howard, was born August 27, 1877, in a home in the country about two miles from Sharpsburg, whither Mr. Heinz had removed. He was educated in Yale, spending his vacations in the business, which he entered actively immediately after his graduation from college. On his father's death he succeeded to the presidency of the company. He married Elizabeth Rust

Birthplace of Henry J. Heinz

"Greenlawn," Residence of Henry J. Heinz, Pittsburgh

HOME AND THE FAMILY FIRESIDE

of Saginaw, Michigan, in 1906, and has two children, H. J. Heinz the 2nd and Rust.

Returning to Sharpsburg in 1879, the family home was maintained there until 1887. Two children were born there, Robert Eugene, who lived less than a month after his birth on May 23, 1882, and Clifford Stanton, born December 30, 1883, who was educated at Lafayette College and is a vice-president of the company. He married Sarah Young of Pittsburgh in 1917, and they have three children.

In 1889, the home in Sharpsburg was given up and a new home was established in Allegheny, now North Side, Pittsburgh. In 1890 the beautiful house and grounds, "Greenlawn," on Penn Avenue, in the section of Pittsburgh known as Homewood, became the family seat. Mr. Heinz' passion for building and developing here found delightful occasion for enlargements and improvements, until, with the years, it had become one of the most attractive residences of a city noted for beautiful dwellings.

In these happy worldly circumstances surrounding his family, Mr. Heinz saw a heavy and grave responsibility lying on himself as a father. With his habit of looking straight at uncomfortable facts, he faced the fact that in too many cases a father's wealth had meant disaster to his sons.

"It should not be so," said he. "The means to provide education and other opportunities should be a great advantage to a boy, not a handicap. It is the father's duty to see to it. Wealth is the father's responsibility, and if his boys go wrong because of it, it is his fault, not theirs."

He taught them that money was only a concrete symbol of success, not a standard. He taught them to think of success only in terms of achievement, ambitious purpose, service rendered to the ultimate degree. It may be accounted as his triumph that in the Heinz house the sons did not talk money, did not think money, and did not think of their father as having money. There had been set before them a greater family pride than the pride of financial prosperity.

They learned the same lesson from both parents—that the only genuine superiority in life comes from superior performance. To

HOME AND THE FAMILY FIRESIDE

Mrs. Heinz, as to him, all show was repugnant. She disliked display in dress or conduct or in any other manifestations. Means meant opportunity for her to engage in ever-widening work for public causes, hospitals, churches. Her excellent health gave her unflagging energy, so, though she was wholly womanly, and a self-sacrificing mother who set her home duty above all, she became a leader in the women's activities of Pittsburgh, fulfilling, among many other duties, the extremely exacting work demanded by her official connection with the Allegheny County Children's Aid Society, whose achievements stand high in the annals of child welfare movements. Her work with the South Side Hospital, her local church and general charity work, all occupied much of her time and interest.

To do more than the average, to do more than might strictly be expected—these ambitions were, somehow, made pleasures in the Heinz household. Mr. Heinz knew too much about children to forget that they must see concrete rewards. So, while they were young, he, like other parents, used the

HOME AND THE FAMILY FIRESIDE

incentive of gifts, money payments for work done, etc. But he spared no pains to make them understand that the reward was not the big factor. He never made the fatal error of bribing his children.

In the same spirit he taught them to save money. He inculcated the habit of saving, not for the pleasure of accumulating, not even primarily as a matter of financial thrift, but as a factor for creating self-restraint and contentment. In his own person he taught contentment every day of his life. He wanted astonishingly little for himself. Indeed, he seemed to have no use for any possession that should be purely his own. He wanted no jewelry or other personal adornment. When he traveled, he laid so little stress on his own comfort that he made no effort to reserve superior accommodations. He was quite content with any hotel room or railroad and steamship berth that he could get. In fact, he often started on an ocean voyage without any previous arrangement for a stateroom, willing to take pot-luck when he got aboard.

Perhaps the hardest part of his work of

HOME AND THE FAMILY FIRESIDE

training his children was the restraint that he had to impose on his own love of giving. He made an art of it. He succeeded in being generous to them, and yet in permitting no gift to seem something that had been lightly come by. Thus, though he was passionately fond of horses, and looked eagerly forward to having his sons share his love and command over them, they were young men before he permitted himself the pleasure of giving them horses of their own. While they were children, they had to be content with a goat-wagon. He promoted them to the ownership of a donkey only, and then to a pony when he knew that they would value the privilege to the utmost. In like manner he made other possessions come as the result of evolution.

Thus, Henry Heinz, the builder, built a family. Side by side, he and his wife were spared to see their offspring emerge from childhood. Side by side, they had the joy of being able, each year, to give more to the causes to which they were devoted. Though he appreciated deeply the marks of esteem that came to him, far greater was his pride in

HOME AND THE FAMILY FIRESIDE

the love that his wife won wherever she went. No one person, except himself, ever knew all she did. Like him, she counted the quiet deed, the unknown service, as the dearest.

She brought succor and happiness into scores of places where she was never known by name. He and she were alike in this—that generous as were their material gifts, the best that they gave was themselves. She gave of herself without stint. Night after night saw her at her sick-beds, where her buoyant, steady temperament brought cheer. It came about that people who, ill and sad, besought their doctors to send for Mrs. Heinz to bring them, as they said, sunshine.

For a quarter century it was given to these two to be with each other on earth in a perfect life. Then, on November 29, 1894, after only a few days' illness from pneumonia, she was taken away. Of the happy married life that was ended thus suddenly no better words can be said than those of the minister, the Reverend E. M. Wood, at her funeral:

> "Twenty-five years ago it was my privilege to join these two lives in the sacred bond

Mrs. Henry J. Heinz

HOME AND THE FAMILY FIRESIDE

of marriage, the binding clause of which bond says, 'Until death do us part'; and not often is it the mournful duty of the same one to stand before the one who is left, and say the sad dissolution of the bond has come at last. But so it is. I have known them in the vicissitudes which have marked and sometimes darkened their lives and their home, and through all such times there has been an abiding faith in the final triumph of truth and right, and they both lived to see a kind and bountiful Providence smile upon them. And her words of cheer and ready helpfulness arched many a dark day with the bow of promise. And now, on that Thanksgiving Day of our nation, when people are expressing their thanks by their offerings, oh, what an offering was this family called upon to give up to God! Of all the costly treasures that have ever been given, there is none so precious as the gift of wife and mother back to God. And this family will not forget how at the last she surrendered herself as the offering with a gracious smile, and with many blessings upon each one of them, as she called them one by one to her bedside; and having given each one of her parting counsel and blessing she left a special blessing for her dear boy far across Atlantic's rolling tide. (*Clarence was attending school in Germany.*) And then, having performed her maternal duty, and expressed with a smile her faith in the glorious future—a faith she had maintained from childhood—she calmly fell asleep in Jesus."

Henry Heinz had no fear of death. He had an abiding faith that the power that cared for him here would never desert him there. He looked upon death as being as natural as life. For the quibbles of theology he had small patience. So he stood erect and unshrinking to take the blow. With a simple and loyal faith he accepted grief as he had accepted blessings. He knew that it was a grief that would never leave him, but he would not let it darken the days of those around him. Twenty-five years passed before the summons came to him also. In all that time he kept the wife of his youth enshrined in his heart's holy of holies, passing through life alone, content with the memory of the first, last and only love of his existence.

XIII
TRAVEL: A REVEALER OF CHARACTER

After ten years of intense application to the building of his business, as he thought, but which turned out to be only the laying of the foundation, Mr. Heinz needed a rest from the sixteen-hour work days to which he was accustomed. In the spring of 1886 he started for a three months' trip to Europe.

To many men such a vacation would have meant a vacant mind, a lolling about in luxurious hotels, with no more mental exercise than was required to learn where the best shows were running and how to reach them. But to him it meant an opportunity for education, which he seized with avidity. He believed that a vacation was not a lazy spell, but a change in the form of one's activity; that the mind is rested by giving it different work to do. So Europe was not a playground, but a university.

He was always striving to supplement the meager teaching of his youth, and no man ever made travel pay a larger return for the

TRAVEL: A REVEALER OF CHARACTER

time and money invested in it. He made travel a school. He had an inquiring mind, an eye from which nothing ever escaped, was never afraid or ashamed to ask questions, and as he went he gathered facts and wisdom, knowledge and understanding.

He kept a very complete record of his observations and experiences during this trip. The entries were made day by day with an enthusiasm and persistency that in themselves reveal character. Of course the value of the information recorded is not to be found in the light it throws on the things he describes, but in the insight which it gives into the mental operations of the man himself. It reveals the man. So we shall follow this travel story of his first trip to Europe, that we may see what things interest him, what sentiments are awakened, what are the habits of his mind—in short, what is his inner life.

Accompanying him were his wife and four children, his sister Mary and a Miss Prager, a family friend. They sailed on May 29, on the steamship "City of Berlin."

The record opens with a mass of detail in respect to the ship and its operation; its size,

TRAVEL: A REVEALER OF CHARACTER

age, speed, tonnage, crew, history, horsepower, mechanical equipment; nothing is omitted. There are notes about the compass, log-line, fog-horn, organization of officers, discipline and duties of the crew; observations as to the sea, its roughness and its smoothness, fogs and the Gulf Stream. From the ship and the sea, his mind passes on to the men "who go down to the sea in ships." The fascination that the sea holds for them is a mystery to him. He cannot understand how they prefer the monotonous, uncertain life of the sea to the absorbing activities of human affairs on land. Still less can he understand how the ever-present perils of the deep do not restrain seafaring men from wickedness and profanity. He concludes that fear of danger is not a potent factor in making men good.

If there was anything in Liverpool worth knowing or seeing that he did not learn or inspect, it must have been wrapped up and laid away in a closet. Its docks and shipping, its population and buildings, its climate, sanitary condition, appearance of streets, its

TRAVEL: A REVEALER OF CHARACTER

tram-cars, horses and carts, industries, customs of business men, all became subjects for comment, with conclusions and observations that clearly show that he has not slavishly followed a guide book, but has gathered his information first hand.

In passing through Bedford, he is reminded of John Bunyan, whose birthplace it was, and takes time to express the opinion that the "Pilgrim's Progress" has "wielded an influence for good in the world that has never waned," and regrets that it is not read as widely as it once was.

His record of London is not the record of a sightseer. It is not the story of a hurried, feverish chase from building to building, from monument to gallery, from historic pile to a modern wonder, absorbing from the official guide so much history that is fiction, so many facts that are not facts, leaving in the end a superficial blur, so confused and indistinct that in a short time every impression has vanished, and the "tourist" can only exclaim, "Oh, yes, we did London—it was great," or like the woman who went through Europe and remembered nothing but the

TRAVEL: A REVEALER OF CHARACTER

wooden bears in Switzerland. It was the careful investigation of a keen mind, the analytical review of all that was learned, the deliberate reaching of conclusions and the painstaking recording of it all.

His first Sunday in London was a full day for a man who was resting, but precisely the kind of a day that he thoroughly enjoyed. His own words picture it best:

"This being Sunday, not forgetting our churchgoing habit, we all drove to the City Road Chapel, the most historic Methodist Church in the world. It was erected by John Wesley in 1778."

After a minute description of the building and the service, and some words of admiration for John and Charles Wesley, he launches forth with enthusiasm into the history and development of Methodism.

Across from City Road Chapel is an old burying-ground. This was visited, and he notes with much satisfaction that he saw the tombs of such worthies as John Bunyan, Oliver Cromwell, Isaac Watt and Susannah Wesley, the mother of John and Charles. The inscription on her tomb was of especial

TRAVEL: A REVEALER OF CHARACTER

interest, so with suitable comment he copies it into his record:

> "In sure and steadfast hope to rise,
> And claim her mansion in the skies,
> A Christian here her flesh laid down,
> The cross exchanging for a crown."

Who knows but what a well-known American orator got his inspiration for a great speech from the last line?

In the afternoon he went to a Free Methodist Sunday School, actuated, he wrote, by "a desire to learn as much as possible concerning the way the religious people of England spent the Sabbath day." He was interested to find that they were studying the International Sunday School lessons, which were used in his school at home, but remarks that they do not use "lesson helps," as in America, confining themselves to the Bible in teaching the lesson.

The evening found him listening to Spurgeon, in the Metropolitan Tabernacle, who impressed him as "the humblest and simplest great man I have ever heard." Thus his first Sunday in London came to a close, a day of busy rest.

TRAVEL: A REVEALER OF CHARACTER

Refreshed by the activities of the Sabbath day, he begins the week with the pursuit of a new line of inquiry. He wishes to know how the world's greatest city cares for its poor, its sick and its helpless. So to Bartholomew Hospital, the oldest in the city, he goes. He learns all about this institution, which at that time was treating annually seventy thousand patients. After pursuing his study of this subject further he takes up another one, a comparison of the methods of and public interest in the Young Men's Christian Association in England with America.

There would be something uncanny about this omnivorous investigator were he to go blithely on his way through Europe with never a thought of his business. We are not surprised, therefore, when we find him devoting a few days to a study of business men and business methods, particularly in the line of his own business. It is only characteristic that he tried his qualities of salesmanship on an old-established English firm. He knew of the famous firm of Fortnum & Mason, Ltd., purveyors to the King and to nobility in

TRAVEL: A REVEALER OF CHARACTER

general, and as he always believed it was necessary to aim high if you are to hit anything, he set out with designs on these very dignified and aristocratic food merchants. He had provided himself with five cases of such of the company's products as he believed would appeal to the English taste. Dressing himself more carefully than usual (although he was always careful about his apparel), and wearing a top hat, he called a cab, had his five cases placed aboard, and ordered the "cabby" to drive to the store of Fortnum & Mason, Ltd., in Piccadilly. He asked for a member of the firm, showed him the goods, explained their merits, and then drew back, figuratively speaking, to brace himself to meet the adverse arguments and objections which he confidently expected. It almost took his breath away when the merchant, without comment, quietly replied: "We will take them all."

Was it the ease with which the sale was made or his appraisal of the magnitude of the English market that set in motion a train of thoughts that ultimately resulted in the establishment of a London Branch House

TRAVEL: A REVEALER OF CHARACTER

nine years later? In any event, the Branch House came, and fought its way against competition, against the traditional conservatism of the English people, against odds so numerous and difficult that no one less than a man with a prophet's vision and a pioneer's faith would have pocketed his loss year after year, with a smile, until the tide turned. But he lived to see his judgment vindicated. The one Branch House has become four, supplemented by a factory, and the British unit is alone doing a business many times as large as the parent house was doing even several years later than when this traveler saw the open door of opportunity. It is significant of his expanding thought of the reach of business that he writes: "Mountains and oceans in this day do not furnish any impassable barrier to the extension of trade." It is his first glimpse of the day when his phrase, "The World our Field," would cease to be a prophecy, and become a reality.

Joseph Parker was the magnet that drew him to the City Temple on the second Sunday in London, where he listened to a sermon

TRAVEL: A REVEALER OF CHARACTER

on "Job's Comforters," and formed this impression: "He is a very peculiar sermonizer, but a good reasoner. He is interesting to listen to, but not to look upon."

Crossing the English Channel, the party soon had its first experience in wrestling with a strange language and stranger customs, but this did not interrupt the same scrutinizing study of Paris that London had received. But he hurried on, because the Fatherland of his sires—Germany—was calling.

At Wittenberg he viewed with reverence the birthplace and cradle of the Reformation, which his early Lutheran training made a Mecca of deepest interest. At Wildbad, in the Black Forest, he observes a type of life which he describes as "most primitive." "Gardening," he writes, "is done on a small scale, and the products hauled to the market in a cart drawn by a cow." Nor does he fail to note the kindness of the peasants and the sweetness and simplicity of rural life.

With his strong religious bent, he never fails to see a church or miss a service, and in this picture of a little Protestant country church in the Black Forest, we have a good

TRAVEL: A REVEALER OF CHARACTER

example of the minuteness of his observations. He had a love for details—whether in or outside of business.

"This is a plain structure of about seventy by one hundred feet, with walls from five to six feet thick, which look as if built to stand for ever. The floors are pine, except the aisles, which are stone. The plain pews are without cushions, and the pulpit is about on a line with the gallery. The worshippers were in plain attire, all carrying their hymn and prayer books. No collection is taken in the church, but on going out the treasurer is at the door with his contribution box, and all are not only expected to, but do, drop something in. The people were very attentive and reverent during the service, and at the close no one was seen speaking to another on passing out."

Leaving Mrs. Heinz and two of the children at Wildbad, he took the two elder boys to Heidelberg, where they entered a private school and acquired considerable knowledge of the language.

Passing on rapidly, many other places in Germany were visited. Thence to Holland, to see the fine vegetable gardens, and finally, with his sister Mary, a visit was paid to Kallstadt, their father's old home. Driving through the little village of the Rhineland, charmed with its vineyards and orchards, everywhere meeting relatives, his record book almost grows into a volume, as with facile pen, he writes of visits with relatives, his talks with them and descriptions of the simple life of the villages. Naturally the old homestead left a deep impress on his memory, and one can imagine the feeling with which he writes: "I slept one night in the old house. It is a stone house of eleven rooms, built by my great-great-grandfather. Many were the strange thoughts that ran through my mind. Imagination was busy picturing the events that may have occurred in this place long ago."

Saying "Good-bye" to the newly-found relatives, who were visited often in later years, he went to Heidelberg for the boys, remained to witness the celebration of the 500th anniversary of the founding of the University, and then the party turned their faces homeward, and in the last entry made

TRAVEL: A REVEALER OF CHARACTER

in the "book of travel" Mr. Heinz wrote, when they came within sight of New York on August 17, there was a mingling of love of country and devotion to God. It was this:

> "Of all banners, ensigns and flags we have seen, none thrills us like the Stars and Stripes. I desire to record my gratitude to the kind Providence that has kept us all in safety and brought us back to our native land, which we love the best."

There can be no doubt that the first trip to foreign lands exercised a great influence upon the character of Mr. Heinz. It gave him a world outlook. His life had been lived under influences largely provincial. He now began to see the significance of events that were transpiring in other lands. And he realized the educative value of travel, when done as he did it—for in closing his record, he wrote:

> "We have seen much and learned much that will tend to broaden and liberalize our views. Travel is one of the best educators, and all that I have gained by my travels I hope to realize in my private life and in business so that my time and expense in turn shall at last inure to the profit of every relation which I sustain to society."

TRAVEL: A REVEALER OF CHARACTER

It was in that spirit that he continued to travel. The impulse of Wanderlust was in his blood. He visited Europe every year except four, between 1890 and 1915. Two times he crossed the Pacific to China and Japan—once around the world—once to the Holy Land, to Egypt several times, and extensively in his own land. He traveled to learn, to broaden his views, to become cosmopolitan in outlook and life, to make himself of greater value to society, and to weave his life's fabric on noble patterns of service. He could say with truth, "I am a part of all I have met." Travel was his university.

The House in Sharpsburg where the Business Began

The House where the Business Began Being Moved
from Sharpsburg to Pittsburgh

XIV
COLLECTING ART AND ANTIQUES

Henry J. Heinz was of the type whom men describe with the words "living in the future." He never arrived at the stage where he wanted to fold his hands and let things stop as they were. He would have considered the world intolerably dull if it had been so ordered that every day should be the same. He was immensely interested in conserving whatever was good. He was more prudent and more cautious than most men. Speculation was foreign to him. He never put a dollar into the stock markets. But he was not conservative in the sense that he wanted the clock to stop because the time suited him as it was.

The future was everything to him. He looked forward to it and welcomed it. In all that he did and thought, he labored for it—for the future of the institution, the future of those in it, the future of his children, the future of the social movements in which he played a part. He made plans for contingencies so far ahead that he knew he could not possibly be alive when they arose.

COLLECTING ART AND ANTIQUES

Yet, side by side with the alert spirit that never wearied of pilotage and exploration, there was a deep and abiding loyalty for old memories and associations. His friends declare that he never forgot anybody of whom he had been fond, or any little episode of his long life that involved a human touch. Time did not obliterate. The passage of the years only deepened and made gracious the fondness of his recollections.

This trait of character gave value in his eyes to many objects outwardly valueless. He prized them as mementoes. Among his smaller belongings after his death were found almost innumerable little keepsakes that dated backward along his whole journey of life—Christmas cards from his parents, souvenirs of wife and children, flotsam and jetsam of a human voyage. Although he had the means to buy for himself almost whatever heart could desire, these were the treasures that he preferred.

He kept them with a spirit of reverence for life's meaning. It was this that led him to save his old desk at which he had toiled when the road was rough. It was this that

COLLECTING ART AND ANTIQUES

made him strive against all odds till he succeeded in moving the old house, "the house where we began," from Sharpsburg to its present honored site in the Pittsburgh group of plant buildings.

From the preservation of personal mementoes, precious only to himself, to such collections as those of his famous ivory carvings and jades, seems like a great and unrelated jump. Really, it was logical evolution, and he advanced toward the result step by step. When he turned to the collecting of art and antiques, he put all his honesty and depth of character into it, and he gathered item after item, not for the sake of piling up rarities, but for the joy and beauty and inspiration that it would bring to others.

The beginning of his career as collector was with miscellaneous objects that were chiefly souvenirs of his trips through the United States. It was a phase of collection that was purely for the sake of association. Among this "association" group were his succeeding collection of Civil War relics and his gatherings of minerals and coins. Most collectors have passed through these stages. Most of them stick there and go no further.

With his widening travels and interests, his ardor increased. He cut down or eliminated most of his past collections, and began to specialize on a few. The first great collection that he made on specialized lines was his collection of watches, antique and historical. The manner in which he entered this field, and gradually made himself expert in it, has been referred to in the first chapter of this book.

It would have given him no pleasure to collect simply by dint of being able to buy what he wanted. His pride was that he had brought the objects together through his own knowledge and study. He would have felt no pride in a collection made for him by hired professionals.

His intention originally in collecting watches was historical. He wanted to gather examples that should portray the entire evolution of watch-making. His bent for getting at the fundamentals of things in business naturally expressed itself in collecting, and he began at the beginning by collecting the

COLLECTING ART AND ANTIQUES

pocket sundials that had been in use before the watch was invented. In the hunt for these comparatively rare objects, he had many adventures of the kind that delight collectors when they get together. He succeeded in obtaining interesting specimens, notably a pocket sundial made in Augsburg in 1618, of which he was extremely proud.

It may be said in a general way that every watch that he added to his cases represented his own progress. It represented all that he had learned while collecting the preceding pieces. In time he possessed a perfectly ordered, historically sound collection that included such characteristic items as a specimen of one of the very earliest attempts, a great mechanism of brass and iron made in Bavaria during the Sixteenth Century. Another unique piece was the watch, more than six inches in diameter, made for the Emperor of China in 1707 by Timotheus Williamson, the famous watchmaker of Fleet Street, London.

In the course of the years that passed during this pursuit, he enlarged on his first idea, and added watches whose value lay not in their exemplification of watchmaking history, but in other historical interest. One of the great prizes that he brought to America, to the envy of all collectors of all nations, was the watch that Admiral Nelson carried in the battle of Trafalgar on October 21, 1805, the day when, after setting the signal, "England expects every man to do his duty," he died for her on his flagship.

The watch, with the letters "N" and "B" engraved on the case ("N" for Nelson and "B" for his ducal title of Bronte) had come on the market in London during one of Mr. Heinz' visits to England. There was no lack of desirous collectors, but the owners set a price on it that made even the most eager hesitate. Mr. Heinz wanted it, but his scruples led him to decide that he was not justified in spending such an amount. He refused to purchase it, but he could not dismiss it from his mind. With the true passion of the collector, he went again and again to look at it. Finally his sister, who was with him, made him happy by urging him not to let the prize escape, and he became its delighted possessor. It was a purchase that he never had to regret,

COLLECTING ART AND ANTIQUES

for it remains one of the valued historic objects of the world.

Commencing with an incentive wholly historical, the beauty of many of the watches that he found gradually became his chief interest, until finally the search for the loveliness of the world became a great and noble part of his life. In this new field, he had to learn not simply new facts, but entirely new significances of human thought and human activity. He had to adjust his own mind to attitudes wholly different from those to which he had been accustomed.

He succeeded in this, too. The art collections that he made are truly his own. He made them as he had made his previous collections, slowly, step by step as he learned. A study of his paintings demonstrates how he proceeded. He tried to avoid errors, but he expected to make them, and he saw to it that each mistake should be turned to account.

A trip to China and Japan in 1902 stimulated his growing admiration for the work of the world's ivory carvers. His collection of these exquisite forms of beauty ultimately became one of the finest in the world. He acquired a knowledge and an understanding of the art that set him high above the ordinary lay collector. In time he became so conversant with the carving arts and crafts of all periods, and of all nations, that there were few great dealers in the world who did not recognize with respect that they had little to tell him.

He particularly enjoyed the work of collecting Japanese carvings, firstly, because of their consummate art and beauty, and secondly, because of the measuring of wits with the adroit Japanese dealers. Mr. Heinz, who was an exceedingly shrewd buyer, was amused by the wiles of the Oriental seller, and admired his talents of salesmanship with the interest of one who himself was an excellent salesman as well as a good buyer.

In his business, where the seller met him fairly, he maintained the principle of looking out for the seller's interest as well as his own. In meeting sharp bargainers on their own ground, as in the case of buying objects for his collections, he reveled in matching shrewdness against shrewdness. Antiques

COLLECTING ART AND ANTIQUES

and objects of art rarely have fixed standards of value. The best experts will make estimates that often vary fantastically. The seller's policy is generally the simple one of getting "all that the traffic will bear." It amused Mr. Heinz to lay a plan of campaign in which he utilized all that he knew of buying and selling and of human nature.

His love for his ivory carvings was, probably, the greatest of his joys as a collector. He found delight in his other collections, many of which were superb, as, for example, the jades and crystals, inro and netsukes and the costume books. But in the presence of the ivory carvings, he was as a passionate worshipper. A large room in his house was remodeled by him to make a fitting frame for them, and here it was his delight to be among them with others to share the pleasure.

He was not of the type of collectors who gather for the sake of private possession. To own anything exclusively for himself never had an appeal to him. Undoubtedly, one of the elements that have given his collections such permanent value is that in making them he was actuated by the thought of how they would inspire many people of many kinds. In the museum that he built on the residence grounds, he welcomed everybody. He even provided a lecturer to describe his collections to any gathering, and especially to young people and the people of the "Heinz business family." At the time of his death he had under construction an addition to his home, which he intended to call the Jade Room, for the better display of the carvings. Some of the finest pieces of the ivory collection, and the watches, were given to the Carnegie Museum for the enjoyment of the public.

He always found rest and peace among them. Many long evenings were spent by him arranging and re-arranging them to bring out their most charming aspects. Losing himself among them, all labors of the day were forgotten, and when he turned away at last from the beloved cases, he was refreshed.

His favorite companion in these silent hours of adoration was a house man, Otto Gruber, who had been in his employ for twenty-two years. He might well have been called "Otto the Silent." He never disturbed

COLLECTING ART AND ANTIQUES

the long vigils among the ivory carvings by a word. He admired them equally with their owner, and was as happy as Mr. Heinz during the evenings given to re-arranging them. He had a set of keys to the cases—a high trust of which he was vastly proud.

For more than three months after Otto died, the ivory cases were not opened, and Mr. Heinz would not disturb a thing that he and Otto had handled together so often. Ever after, he kept a picture of the faithful employee on the wall of his room.

XV

RELIGION AND SUNDAY SCHOOL WORK

ONE of the Pittsburgh newspapers commenced its article announcing his death with these words: "Henry J. Heinz, churchman, philanthropist, manufacturer, founder and president of H. J. Heinz Company." The emphasis was placed correctly when he was described first as "churchman."

The Board of Trustees of the University of Pittsburgh, in the resolution of sorrow for his death, said: "He cared for art, for beauty, for education, for good citizenship, for civic betterment, for the well-being of people; he cared for the great business of which he was the creator; he cared supremely for his family, for his country and for other countries also, but the real passion of his life was religion."

In the opening paragraph of his will, he declared: "Looking forward to the time when my earthly career shall end, I desire to set forth at the very beginning of this will,

RELIGION AND SUNDAY SCHOOL WORK

as the most important item in it, a confession of my faith in Jesus Christ as my Saviour. I also desire to bear witness to the fact that throughout my life, in which there were the usual joys and sorrows, I have been wonderfully sustained by my faith in God through Jesus Christ. This legacy was left me by my sacred mother, who was a woman of strong faith, and to it I attribute any success I may have attained during my life."

It was his mother who said to him in his youth: "Henry, I have only one piece of advice to give you about your religion. Do not make it so narrow that it will be unattractive to others, and do not make it so broad that you leave yourself no foundation on which to stand."

His religion was a base on which he stood foursquare——not once a week, but seven days a week, in business and out of business. But it was its spirit that he cared for, and not ostentation of it. He offered it to men, but forced it on none. His understanding and respect went out to all creeds.

In his youth he was an adherent of the Lutheran Church, in which he had been

RELIGION AND SUNDAY SCHOOL WORK

brought up. When he married, his wife being a United Presbyterian, they compromised their differences of view as to denomination by uniting with the Methodist Episcopal Church, of which the Reverend E. M. Wood, who had married them, was pastor. In 1870 Mr. Heinz became a steward, and in 1871 was chosen Sunday School superintendent and trustee.

A new church had been erected and was to be dedicated soon after he became a member. There was a debt of $8000 to be provided for. A meeting of the officials was held, at which he was present because he was a steward. It was decided to ask, from those present, for five subscriptions of two hundred dollars each. Most of the persons present were of small means, and subscriptions came slowly. But finally four were made. Mr. Heinz was a young man, recently married, and struggling to get a foothold in business. He did some serious thinking as the subscriptions were being taken. He realized that from a practical business point of view he would not be justified in pledging two hundred dollars, when he did not have it or know where he could get it. On the other hand, he recalled a pledge he had made to himself when he entered upon religious life, to shirk no duty and to contribute his share of the expense of the work of the church. He balanced the two points of view for a moment—business prudence versus religious duty—and ended the matter by making the subscription of $200. When his mother learned of it, her sense of prudence and economy was shocked, pious though she was, and she gently chided him. He told her that he was happy in what he had done, as he had obeyed his resolution, adding, "If the Lord wants me to do this, he will show me the way to make good my pledge."

The following Monday evening there was a meeting of a building and loan association, of which he was a member. It was the custom to select by lot from the members, once a month, five who would be privileged to borrow the money paid in during the month. Any member selected who did not wish to borrow immediately could sell his right to another, at a premium which was usually $20 a share.

Henry J. Heinz with Cradle Roll Representatives at State Sunday School Convention, York, Penna., 1916

RELIGION AND SUNDAY SCHOOL WORK

The first name drawn was that of Mr. Heinz. As he arose to state that he did not wish to borrow the money, another member offered him $21 a share for the privilege. As he held ten shares, this meant $210. It flashed into his mind that here was the way to meet his pledge to the church, and the offer was quickly accepted. Although his mother lived nearly a mile away, and it was after eleven o'clock at night, he hurried to his mother's home, to exclaim: "Mother, you remember my pledge to the church? Well, the Lord has provided a way to meet it," and he told the story. The circumstance deeply impressed him, gave a set to his conviction that when Christian duty called it was his business to respond, whether he could always see the way to the end or not, and strengthened him in his purpose, to which he adhered during all his life, to put his trust in a Higher Power.

In the following year they decided to leave their church owing to a split in the congregation over the question of a choice of ministers and they joined the Grace Methodist Protestant Church near their home. It was

RELIGION AND SUNDAY SCHOOL WORK

a small church with membership largely of the kind of people for whom he always had the greatest liking—the kind often referred to as "plain people." No church relation was more happy and fruitful than the period of almost twenty years during which he worshipped with this congregation. Even after he removed to another part of the city, he often went there. On the Sunday immediately before he was seized with his fatal illness, he attended its service.

After removal to the East End of Pittsburgh, his children united with the Presbyterian Church and he transferred his own membership to that denomination, joining the East Liberty Presbyterian Church, where his membership continued till death.

Lutheran, Methodist Episcopal, Methodist Protestant, Presbyterian—these many denominational choices were not vacillations. He was not trying different creeds and form to see which he would like best. They meant that he was not fettered by denominationalism. It was the inner life, not the outer form, that he cared for. The man who "did justly, loved mercy and walked humbly with God"

RELIGION AND SUNDAY SCHOOL WORK

was in his view a Christian whether he subscribed to all the rules of creed or not.

His business was a monument worthy of his service, but his service for his Master is a greater monument than his business.

One often hears it said that a business man, at least one who deals with other than small affairs, cannot be a Christian. It is affirmed that there is an irreconcilable incompatibility between the principles of business and the teachings of Christ. The life of such a man as Mr. Heinz is an answer to that theory. He made a success of his business; he made a success of his Christian living. There was no lack of harmony between them. His Christian life was a help to him in his business. His business enabled him to make his Christian life effective in ways of practical service to others.

From earliest manhood he believed that the Sunday School was the supremely useful instrumentality for the instruction of those whom the church is set to reach and rear; and to the Sunday School movement, local, national and international, he gave altogether sixty-four years of unbroken and unwearied work. In many respects, he made it the leading labor of his life.

A few months before his death he said:

> "From my early boyhood I have been a member of the Sunday School. In my early twenties, I was a teacher; at twenty-six, superintendent of a village school. In middle life I became identified with the organized Sunday School work.
>
> "To the child, the Sunday School is a great source from which to obtain life's principles.
>
> "To the young man or young woman, either as scholar or teacher, it pays the greatest reward possible for the time and means invested.
>
> "To one in middle life it is a constant inspiration, while in ripe years it is the greatest influence in sustaining one's hope and faith in immortality.
>
> "To my mind, the Sunday School is the world's greatest living force for character building and good citizenship. It has paid me the largest dividends of any investment I ever made. I bear testimony that in my own life the Sunday School has been an influence and an inspiration second only to that of a consecrated mother."

RELIGION AND SUNDAY SCHOOL WORK

This testimony was based on an experience beginning in 1854 and continuing to 1919 as shown by the record that follows:

IN LOCAL SCHOOL

Scholar . . . . 12 years 1854–1866
Secretary, Treasurer, Teacher and Superintendent . . 25 years 1870–1895

IN ORGANIZATION WORK
ALLEGHENY COUNTY SABBATH SCHOOL ASSOCIATION

Director . . . . 26 years 1893–1919
President . . . . 4 years 1898–1902

PENNSYLVANIA STATE SABBATH SCHOOL ASSOCIATION

Director . . . . 24 years 1895–1919
President . . . . 13 years 1906–1919

INTERNATIONAL SUNDAY SCHOOL ASSOCIATION

Member of Executive Committee . . 17 years 1902–1919
Vice-President . . 1 year 1918–1919

WORLD'S SUNDAY SCHOOL ASSOCIATION

Member Executive Committee . . 15 years 1904–1919
Chairman Executive Committee . . 6 years 1913–1919

RELIGION AND SUNDAY SCHOOL WORK

His Sunday School apprenticeship was as a member of the pastor's class in the Lutheran Sunday School of Sharpsburg. His election as superintendent in the Methodist Episcopal Church School was the beginning of twenty-five years of valuable work in the local Sunday School field. He was working sixteen hours and more in his business, but he managed to give so much time and energy to the superintendent's office that he inspired pastor, teachers and pupils alike. After Mr. Heinz' death, a Sunday School Superintendent told how, when he was a small boy, Mr. Heinz had given him books and other help. "This was at the busiest time of his career," he said, "when he was laying the foundations of his business, yet he had time to talk to a boy of eight years about his affairs and future, and he had time to talk to boys and girls in our Sunday School."

When organized Sunday School work began to develop, he saw its possibilities. He became a member of the Board of Directors of the Allegheny County Sabbath School Association, and five years later, in 1898,

RELIGION AND SUNDAY SCHOOL WORK

became president, holding office for four successive yearly terms. A strong organization was built up. Men of business influence were attracted to the association. Headquarters were established in a dignified office building. He brought a specialist from Minneapolis to organize a survey, or, as it was called then, a house-to-house canvass, to find out what the field for Sunday School work in Pittsburgh was—how many children were not in the Sunday School, how many people were unattached to any church, etc.

The people to do the work were recruited among the city's Sunday Schools. Two thousand canvassers were drilled and trained. Co-operation of the pastors of all the churches was obtained. The interest of the press was awakened, in order to help the work by making the people sympathetic toward it. On a day in April, 1899, the efforts resulted in a canvass of half a million people, living in 83,000 homes, and a great mass of religious data was thereafter available to all those interested in church movements.

At the end of the canvass, he gave a banquet to the directors and presidents of the forty-two districts into which the county had been divided. He said in his address:

> "We realize more and more our dependence upon the great head of the church. We have all the time there is, and we are responsible to the Maker and Giver of time, as to how we use it. There can be no more profitable way of spending it than to teach, encourage and inspire the youth of our county during their impressionable years. Horace Mann once said: 'When anything is growing, one former is worth a thousand reformers.' We love the Sunday School work more and more, because we realize its possibilities, since the young men and women of today will not only be the fathers and mothers of the present generation, but of generations to come. We have succeeded marvelously well in our house-to-house visitation of our city. We have not only placed our Protestant denominations in position to do better and more effective work, but have secured data that will enable the Catholic Church to do the same. We each do our work in our own way, but both stand for nothing less than character building and good citizenship."

RELIGION AND SUNDAY SCHOOL WORK

In 1895 a business trip took him to Williamsport, Pennsylvania, where the Pennsylvania State Sabbath School Association was holding its convention. He entered the hall just as John Wanamaker, then serving his first year as president, was appealing for subscriptions to meet a deficit of $600, concluding with the declaration that unless a budget system was adopted and the association kept free from debt, he would never attend another convention.

Mr. Heinz, though a stranger, and only a chance visitor, arose and said: "Mr. President, if you will stand by that principle, and pay as you go, and not use the time of your conventions in raising deficits, you may put me down for $100."

When asked for his name, he wrote his initials on a slip and passed it to the platform, saying that he would give his name to the teller later. He had wished to help, not to thrust his personality forward. The incident, however, led to his election to the executive committee, starting a service of twenty-four years in the state work, nine of which were as chairman of the executive

RELIGION AND SUNDAY SCHOOL WORK

committee, and thirteen years as president of the association, following Mr. Wanamaker, who retired after twelve years of office, nominating Mr. Heinz as his successor.

During more than twenty years, he traveled across the State of Pennsylvania, from Pittsburgh to Philadelphia, once a month, ten months in the year, except when absent from the United States, to be present at the monthly meeting of the directors of the State Association.

There was steady expansion of the work, and the budget necessarily grew, but good organization and sustained enthusiasm admirably facilitated financing. At one time, something like fifteen counties failed to pledge anything toward the budget. Mr. Heinz arose and said that no county should appear on the association books with nothing to its credit. "If you will permit me," he added, "I will contribute $25 for each county that has not responded." The general secretary of the association, Mr. Landes, resolved to ask these counties to pay the pledges made by Mr. Heinz. He went into

RELIGION AND SUNDAY SCHOOL WORK

one, and was told: "Well, the folks are pretty poor down here. Mr. Heinz has a good deal of money. I guess we'll let him pay for us."

Mr. Landes reported to Mr. Heinz, who laughed and replied: "I will guarantee that won't happen again. They will be ashamed." He was right. Within two years every county was offering and meeting its pledges, and many increased the amounts year after year.

During his administration, with the capable and energetic men who co-operated with him, the association became owner of the splendid property on Arch Street, Philadelphia, being the first Sunday School Association in the world to possess its own headquarters building. The financial receipts increased from $12,000 a year in 1903 to $34,000 a year in 1918. The membership of adult Bible classes reached 372,000. The Teacher Training Department, esteemed of vital importance by him, exceeded that of any other state in the number of teachers graduated. In general, the Pennsylvania State Sabbath School Association was brought to the place where it was conceded

RELIGION AND SUNDAY SCHOOL WORK

to lead all the states in Sunday School work. Each of the sixty-seven counties today maintains an annual convention.

In 1899 he was made the representative of Pennsylvania on the Executive Committee of the International Sunday School Association, embracing the North American continent. Later he became a trustee, and in 1918 a vice-president.

His first vision of the world-wide possibilities of the Sunday School came to him while traveling with his son in the Orient, in 1902, when, as the unofficial representative of a Mission Board, he visited missions, and at the request of certain Sunday School leaders also investigated the status of Sunday School work.

In his report, read at the Denver convention of the International Association, he said: "Japan is the key to the Orient. The work done through this Sunday School movement and through the missionaries in this ambitious, progressive country will be looked upon with favor by the neighboring people of Korea and China. It is 'judicious advertising' of the great Sunday School

RELIGION AND SUNDAY SCHOOL WORK

movement, destined to become world-wide in its scope and of blessed results."

At the Toronto convention in 1905 he expressed his faith in the Japanese, pointed to the strategy of winning Japan for the Sunday School, and concluded by pledging $1000 a year for three years toward the support of a worker in that country.

Frank L. Brown was delegated to go to Japan and promote the organization of the Japanese National Sunday School Association. He reported to the convention of 1907 in Rome, when it was decided to organize the World's Sunday School Association for world-wide work, and to provide for a Sunday School Missionary tour around the world to make a survey.

In 1913, at the head of twenty-nine business men and Sunday School experts, Mr. Heinz led the way to the Orient, and devoted five months to a campaign through Japan, Korea and China, visiting more than seventy cities, meeting statesmen and others of prominence, and holding daily conferences and meetings. Frank L. Brown has described this trip in his book, "The Tour of the Orient."

The tour party proceeded to the convention of the World's Association which met in Zurich in June, 1913. Mr. Heinz was hailed as a Christian statesman and leader, and chosen chairman of the Executive Committee, an international honor that well crowned his Sunday School career of more than half a century.

Returning from his around-the-world trip, he built a Sunday School office at his residence and employed a Sunday School secretary to enable him to push the work incumbent on his new position. The party had made so favorable an impression in Japan that the convention for 1916 was invited to Tokio, but the world war caused postponement.

No small part of every day was devoted ungrudgingly to what he had come to regard as an enterprise worthy of his best. In the midst of his activity and planning, with railroad tickets in his pocket to go to New York for a conference on the world-work and on the Tokio convention, he was smitten with

RELIGION AND SUNDAY SCHOOL WORK

pneumonia; and on May 14, 1919, the wires sent the tidings around the world that his place was vacant.

With characteristic foresight, that his passing should not deprive the work he loved of some contribution from his hand, he had made bequests in his will:

> To the Allegheny County Sabbath School Association . . . . $ 50,000
> To the Pennsylvania State Sabbath School Association 75,000
> To the International Sunday School Association 75,000
> To the World's Sunday School Association 100,000

He provided that in each case the sum be invested in investments legal for trustees, the income to be used for the regular work of the association as it shall deem proper.

He bequeathed $250,000 to the University of Pittsburgh, in memory of his mother, to be used for religious training of the students—$150,000 to be used for the erection of a building, and $100,000 for the maintenance of a chair to be devoted to the training of Sunday School teachers and instructors in

Sunday School work generally. He wrote: "I am led to make this provision because of my appreciation of the value of teacher-training work conducted by the Pennsylvania State Sabbath School Association."

His death brought expressions of sorrow and dismay from all parts of the world where men were engaged in the work that he had so long and so enthusiastically fathered. In scores of solemn memorial services there was recognition of his sixty-four years of faithful effort for the building of character in the youth of his own land and of other lands. A tender demonstration of affection was the journey of a representative of the two hundred thousand Japanese Sunday School members to Pittsburgh, to lay a wreath on the tomb of the man who had taken to his heart the children of Japan.

Sarah Heinz House. Built by Henry J. Heinz as a Memorial to His Wife

XVI
CITIZEN

THE measure of worthiness is helpfulness. We have learned to test men not by birth, nor by intellectual power, nor by wealth, but by service. Ancestry is noble if the good survives in him who boasts of his forebears. Intellectual force is worthy if it can escape from conceit. Wealth is not to be despised if it is untainted and consecrated. But they are sunk into insignificance when character is considered; for character is the child of self-denial and love. The man who lives for others, and who has a heart big enough to take all men into its living sympathies—he is the man who has a real conception of true citizenship.

His idea of citizenship was something to be expressed not merely in political directions. As he did not separate his religious life, his business life and his home life, so he did not set his duties of citizenship apart. They meant to him citizenship in all affairs of life, every day and all day, year in and year out.

CITIZEN

There was no man more proud of being a citizen of the Republic, and no man more loyal to Nation, State and City. His way of showing it was to perform those duties that were next to his hand; and because his way of service was to put his own shoulder to the wheel, his mind was most given to those betterments that can be brought about by men acting on and with each other directly in the every-day occupations of life. Therefore, most of the public and semi-public offices that he filled were offices that would enable him to exercise personal influence and give personal labor. His extraordinary vital energy enabled him to carry these additional duties as briskly as if each were the only one. He never grew old enough to be willing to act as figure-head.

He gave time and energy to the board of the Chamber of Commerce and similar organizations. He served as director in banks and other institutions where his chief or only incentive was the responsibility of trusteeship. Besides his widely branching duties in church work and the social and community work related to it, he was a member of the

CITIZEN

board of the Western Pennsylvania Hospital, the Tuberculosis League, and many other such public services. Early in his business life he became director and a moving spirit in the Western Pennsylvania Exposition Society, which did so much for community benefit and during the last fifteen years of his life he was its vice-president.

He had small fondness for political quarrels, but he never shirked a fight when one was called for. One of these political battles was for the annexation of Allegheny to Pittsburgh, in the Greater Pittsburgh campaign of 1905. The political machine that ruled Allegheny was red hot against it, and it had power which Mr. Heinz did not underestimate. He knew very well that the location of the Heinz plant in Allegheny rendered him open to reprisals in all forms, from oppressive taxation to other punitive measures. Despite this, he took the chairmanship of a meeting of those Allegheny citizens who favored the Greater Pittsburgh legislation, and amid menacing objections from adherents of Allegheny office-holders, he succeeded in holding the meeting together till it had adopted a resolution calling on the legislature to pass the bill. So well was this demand fortified by the names of prominent business men that this meeting always has been credited with having done invaluable work for the success of the movement. Mr. Heinz had been a leader in the Greater Pittsburgh movement for years and had served on the central committee.

Another hard civic fight was his fight against evil, organized and unorganized, when he decided to clean up a dwelling district near the Heinz plant, and make it fit for laboring people of small earning power to live in. It was known as a "red light" district, and real-estate men, as well as police and other city officials, told him that he was undertaking an impossible task.

He purchased quietly till, in the course of two years, he possessed several hundred properties. As the regular real-estate men were so sure that he could not succeed, he established his own real-estate department, opening two offices with staffs of office men and repair men. Trained investigators, aided at times by detectives hired by him, were sent to get

CITIZEN

the facts necessary to drive out objectionable tenants and to make sure of good ones in their place. "Go back through their records for fifteen years, if necessary," he told them, "so that we'll be sure of every tenant."

When he got the right tenants, he kept them. He kept them by the simple device of making repairs before they were requested, and making improvements, big and little, which no tenant of that class ever would have dreamed of getting. The word was passed around. The district became a home district of decent people. Its whole appearance was changed. And greatly to his delight, he was able to demonstrate to the doubting Thomases that it worked out practically as well as ethically. Before his time, the nature of the tenancy had caused fluctuating habitation with a vacancy of about twenty per cent, added to which was the loss of rents from those who flitted without notice. The net income from the properties, despite the fact that nothing or next to nothing had been expended on them for repairs, had been less than one per cent. Mr. Heinz could point to a record of no vacancies at all, rentals paid regularly, and a net income of five or six percent, all created by management, to the benefit of landlord and tenants, both.

He was sixty-five years old when he thus entered a business new to him, and successfully devised a way of his own to conduct it. While he still was building the district up, he was called upon to become chairman of the Pittsburgh Flood Commission, to seek a definite method for controlling the rivers whose erratic behavior so often made wide destruction. He accepted enthusiastically. It was a service that brought into play all those qualities predominant in him—hatred of waste, analytical study for basic causes, constructiveness. Hundreds of thousands of dollars were raised by public subscription to augment the appropriations from city, county and state. At his own expense he went to Europe to study flood-control, returning with a mass of invaluable reports and technical information. A complete survey was made of the watersheds of the Ohio and the Allegheny with their tributaries. Great manufacturers and merchants, real-estate owners and engineers, all joined as members of the commission to make it a work as thorough as any ever done in the United States.

The plan, as finally presented, provided for a radical and definite elimination of flood-water, but necessarily it was a plan that went far beyond what the City of Pittsburgh, or even the State of Pennsylvania, could do alone, because the watersheds lay, in part, in other states. The magnitude of the project was so enormous that its sponsors knew very well that many years must pass before even a beginning could be made, for aside from the financial problem, the legal aspects demanded action by the Federal Government as well as co-operation from various neighboring states. Mr. Heinz hardly expected to see the work begun in his lifetime, but he took great pride in the report and the plans, feeling that ultimately they should lead to a colossal modern work of reclamation and conservation which will be a monument to American engineering science and vision.

Another communal activity that gave him enduring happiness was the work of the

CITIZEN

Western Pennsylvania Exposition Society, which, in its time, did great service for community improvement. He was particularly interested in its musical program, for, though he was without musical training, he had a vivid perception of the cultural influence of music. As the price of admission to the whole Exposition (which lasted two months each year) was only twenty-five cents, he saw the opportunity for bringing classical music and great artists to the people. He was not afraid of "going over their heads."

Colonel J. M. Schoonmaker, who was chairman of the Music Committee, in telling how Mr. Heinz inspired the idea of offering a type of music higher than the customary bands, told this story: "The first great artist we had was Materna. She had a magnificent voice, there was a great audience, and she sang most beautifully. But it was plain to me that her music was away above the heads of the people. I tried to start the applause, but it did not draw much. There were two great big fellows near me who didn't applaud, and I heard one say: 'Oh ———, I'd rather hear ———,' mentioning a very ordinary singer of popular songs. I told my story to Mr. Heinz, saying I was afraid that we had made a big mistake. He smiled and said: 'Go ahead. We will get a music-loving community by and by. We will educate the people up to good music.' We took his advice, and it will be recollected what good music we had at the Exposition, and the many great artists who appeared. The people enjoyed Damrosch, for instance, for a whole afternoon or evening for twenty-five cents instead of two dollars and fifty cents. A musical atmosphere, with the refinements that go with it, grew up in our community; and it was due largely to Mr. Heinz' nerve and vision."

A child problem that was very close to him was that of the children in the district around the plant—not merely in the properties owned by him, but in the whole area. Their pleasures and opportunities were pitiably small, for their parents were mostly of the unskilled laboring class. He started a canvass of the number of children, their ages and other facts, to get the basis for a plan. While he was revolving various ideas, he had an interesting little psychological experience. He dreamed that his son Howard, then at Yale, had come to him with a proposal to undertake this community task.

It was, of course, wholly logical that to a mind occupied with the problem there should come such a solution in a dream, for he and his son had long been intimately united in thoughts and purposes. There was, however, a coincidence that gave it a touch of the unusual. A day or two after the dream, he received a letter from Yale, in which the son asked permission to start the club work for boys in the factory neighborhood.

In 1901 Howard Heinz began in what he described later as "a couple of rooms, a kitchen, and a bath tub." It was named "The Covode House," in memory of Jacob Covode of Sharpsburg, who had been Mr. Heinz' staunch friend when friendship was sorely needed back in the panic of '76. The work began with a few boys gathered from the alleys. It grew so fast, its young founder could hardly keep up with it. His father pursued his usual strategy—allowed him to bear all the responsibility, acted as if he did

CITIZEN

not see the duties and labors piling up, and yet managed to participate in the club life and to supply the necessary means without undermining initiative. In fact, the history of that beginning, told in all its smaller details, would make an illuminating chapter in the science of social experiments.

The two rooms grew to a couple of moderately sized buildings. Several hundred boys were being looked after, and the staff had grown from the one young college man to a number of workers. When the idea of a similar club for girls presented itself as the next stage in development, Mr. Heinz perceived that the opportunity had arrived for carrying out a deep, fond intention—that of erecting a memorial to his departed wife that should truly typify what her life had represented. There could be none more truly and beautifully expressive of her, whose great heart had gone out to every unfortunate child, than a building to house fittingly and nobly the work that her son had founded.

So it was that there arose, on the corner of Ohio and Heinz Streets, a building named

CITIZEN

SARAH HEINZ HOUSE, bearing on its front a tablet with the inscription:

DEDICATED TO
YOUTH   RECREATION
CHARACTER SERVICE

One hundred and twenty-five feet long and sixty feet deep, its three stories and basement contain club rooms, game rooms, library, gymnasium, swimming pool and all other requirements of a modern, thoroughly equipped social settlement house.

So happily designed that it expresses the grace and quiet beauty of its purpose, it stands as a memorial to a good woman and also as an embodiment of family citizenship. As Mr. Heinz said at the time of its dedication on June 6, 1915:

> "This is a happy day to me. I have looked forward to the erection of some such house as this for a long time. For years I held the corner lot here in reserve for this purpose. As my ideas grew more definite, I realized that the corner lot would be too small. I saw it would be necessary to buy adjoining houses and lots, and clear away the houses to give the room needed.

CITIZEN

There was a bit of selfishness in it, too, I admit. The pleasure received in carrying out a conception is proportioned to the completeness with which the embodiment of the ideal corresponds to the ideal itself. This sort of pleasure is the fountain at which youth is renewed. I desire to grow younger as the years go by. Why should I not receive the enjoyment that comes from working to realize a building so complete that it would not fall short of the ideal that inspired its erection? This thought influenced me so much that I took a year longer in planning and constructing this building than first intended. I studied other buildings designed for a similar purpose. I desired that this building would compare with the best in the land, and be as well adapted to its purpose as human wisdom could make it.

"I do not know what percentage of the young people connected with this work is Protestant or what percentage is Catholic. Furthermore, I do not want to know. No sectarian bias will influence the work of this institution. We want to make this a factory for character building and good citizenship. It is our desire to surround the boys and girls of this neighborhood with such good influences that they will never

CITIZEN

want to depart from the right paths. Good citizenship is the purpose that we shall keep in view. Character, which is the outgrowth of honor, will be the goal of our endeavors."

His conception of his duty as a citizen was not narrowed to his own city. In one instance it was wide enough to reach out beyond his country and include a foreign land. He always deprecated the jingoism displayed by the yellow press in the discussion of the relations between our country and Japan. His visit to Japan in 1913 with the Sunday School Commission was made an occasion to put to the front at every opportunity the thought of peace between the countries. As more than seventy cities were visited and contact had with leading citizens, he saw an opportunity to say a word for peace, and it was said with a sincerity that brought similar response from such men as Count Okuma, later premier; Baron (now Viscount) Shibusawa; and other men of high position who guided public opinion in Japan. The key-note of the many addresses he made on this tour was that sounded in an

CITIZEN

address before the Chamber of Commerce at Tokio, at a banquet given in honor of the American guests, when he said: "We come to you with a message of good-will and friendship. In our relations with you as a nation our Republic has stood for peace, from the days of Commodore Perry, to whom you opened your ports, to the time of President Roosevelt and the treaty of Portsmouth, and of President Taft, who has sought to make war between great nations impossible. And this has been the attitude of your great Empire, whose three wars in the last two centuries have been in self-defense and for national honor. At times agitators have sought to disturb our peaceful relations, but the American people are determined that our friendship shall remain undisturbed."

Dinner Tendered to Henry J. Heinz on His Seventieth Birthday

XVII

READING THE RECORD

THE life of Henry J. Heinz was a long life, and it was a life whose record was open for all men to read. When he passed, they rendered their verdict in the tongues of many races, and from many aspects of human thought. But anywhere and everywhere it was the same. And in no way was it different from the verdicts that men had uttered while he still lived.

For his seventieth birthday some old friends, with his son Howard, arranged a surprise birthday party with a guest for each of his years. On that evening of October 11, 1914, he looked along a flower-decked room and saw seventy such men as any one, no matter what honors had ever come to him, might well feel proud to see assembled.

From those who knew him most closely —his fellow directors in the company, who had dealt with him daily in the stress of circumstance—came the testimony, presented

READING THE RECORD

in a form whose beauty of design was worthy of the contents:

> "You are not living with the memories of the past but are using the opportunities of the present to realize the promises of the future; this keeps you young at heart. You have put nothing before honor, duty and service, and happiness has been the result. You have measured not the vanity of life, but its importance, facing its difficulties with courage. You have seen cherished ambitions realized. While disappointments and sorrows have been your portion at times, they did not crush your hope or fill your heart with fear, or cause you to lose faith in yourself, your fellow men and your God. Thus have your years been crowned with the best that life can bring. As you face the future, your life will be an inspiration to all upon whom its light may shine, teaching them in its gentleness and kindness the wisdom and strength and peace of a well-ordered life that has come naturally and progressively to its full fruition."

As the evening went on, man after man arose and gave his tribute—Dr. John A. Brashear, "Pennsylvania's foremost citizen," world famous for his work in science and astronomy, but known to all Pittsburgh as

READING THE RECORD

"Uncle John"; Colonel Samuel Harden Church, President of Carnegie Institute; Justice W. P. Potter of the Supreme Court of Pennsylvania; Dr. George W. Bailey, a prominent merchant of Philadelphia; the Honorable Thomas H. Murray; Dr. D. S. Stephens of Kansas City; Francis J. Torrance; D. P. Black; James W. Kinnear; A. J. Kelly; the Reverend Dr. Frank W. Sneed, his pastor. Willis F. McCook, a leader of the Pittsburgh bar, presented him with a birthday book, a beautiful example of book art, which contained a greeting to which each guest appended his signature.

From Governor Brumbaugh of the State of Pennsylvania came the written message, addressed to Howard Heinz: "You little know how much your good father is loved. His splendid enthusiasm, his fine business insight, his manly modesty, his love for others, and, above all, his fine Christian character, make him a great leader and one of Pennsylvania's truly noble citizens."

John Wanamaker, addressing Mr. Heinz as "My dear long-time friend," wrote: "However the years may count up, neither time nor multiplying duties faithfully done by you seem to make you older. Keep straight on, dear man of infinite kindness, of modest generosity and manly friendships, and noble Christian testimony, and great shall be your reward on earth as well as in Heaven."

Hardly able to command his feelings or voice, Mr. Heinz responded to these testimonials:

> "In a sense, I have done very little. I have tried to inspire a little in others because I believe in humanity. I believe in men. There are so few dishonest people in the world that all it has been necessary for me to do has been simply to keep an eye on the few who need watching, and then trust everyone else.
>
> "It has not been necessary for me to do much. I could always go away from home knowing that my splendid partners and business associates would do better when I was away than when I was at home. When you have your partners who can do these things, and do them so much better, what is the use of your doing them? No institution of any kind ever was made great by any one man. You and I would not be the men we are today had it not been

READING THE RECORD

for the men who have helped us. This is my faith.

"Our birthdays after fifty come and pass too rapidly. Andrew Carnegie once said that the forties were the years of meditation. I would add to this, that the fifties and the later years are the years of philosophy. If we do not by this time philosophize, we are not getting out of life what we might.

"There are three things men should do in this life, and they are about all there is to life. The first is to plan for the comfort of our loved ones, the second is to so live that we may enjoy the respect, the esteem and the confidence of our fellow men. Last, but not least, is to do just one greater thing—live for the hereafter."

He declared that night that he felt as if he were no more than forty; and for five years following he continued to work and live as if he did, indeed, enjoy a gift of unending youth.

In the end of January, 1919, he went to Florida, taking with him his old friend, Bishop Joseph F. Hartzell, who had long served as Bishop for Africa of the Methodist

Episcopal Church. He returned in April, and all his friends remarked his physical vigor and his mental and spiritual vivacity. On May 9, after luncheon with the directors at the plant, he learned that an old salesman was in, sent for him and enjoyed one of the reminiscent visits and chats that he loved.

He awoke on Saturday with a slight cold. His physician advised him to stay in his room, but thought he should be well enough by Sunday night to leave for New York, where he meant to attend a meeting of the Executive Committee of the World's Sunday School Association.

On Sunday pneumonia developed. He became rapidly worse, with only a short period of improvement on Tuesday, and at four o'clock on the next afternoon, May 14th, the end came, in his seventy-fifth year. The funeral services, held in the East Liberty Presbyterian Church, were conducted by his pastor, Dr. Frank W. Sneed, and his friend, Bishop Hartzell. He was laid away in Homewood Cemetery.

The news of his death was received throughout the world as tidings of a genuine

Memorial Erected by Employees of H. J. Heinz Company in Memory of the Founder

READING THE RECORD

loss. From Tokio, Japan, came a cable dispatch signed by the triumvirate of great Japanese, Okuma, Shibusawa and Saketani, which epitomized the general feeling in the four words: "Your loss, world's loss." In New York, at the meeting of the World's Sunday School Association committee that he had planned to attend, John Wanamaker said with tears: "A great man is gone." "A whole company will have to be called to fill the void left by his going away," said one of the newspapers.

There were many memorial meetings, and four of these, of which one was in Tokio, were great public ones attended by such assemblages as are drawn only by public occasions that stir men deeply. Those who had known him longest and most closely—the company's employees—held a meeting in the auditorium of the plant, where there was a wonderful, spontaneous outpouring of affection. Its tenor can be best expressed in the words of the First Vice-President of the Company, Sebastian Mueller: "He was a father to us all. He reared us into manhood,

READING THE RECORD

and he guided us with a kind and gentle spirit."

There is no intention of reproducing here, or even quoting from the tributes of respect, admiration, gratitude and affection that came by one impulse from all parts of the world. If they were combined, they would make a volume far larger than this which tells the story of the life that brought forth these testimonials.

We know of no more fitting way to conclude the history of that faithful and unpretentious life than with just three short quotations.

Two are from workingmen. A simple old laborer of the plant, who stood unobtrusively near the door of the crowded plant auditorium during the employees' memorial meeting, turned away when it was over and said, addressing nobody in particular: "Well they told no lies about him. He was an honest man, and he was my best friend."

"I have lost the best friend I ever had," said another workingman who had served a quarter century in a Western branch.

READING THE RECORD

When his body lay coffined at home, a child came shyly to the door and offered a handful of wayside blossoms. "He was always doing so much for us," she said.